Your Dreams Don't Die... They Haunt You

Your Dreams Don't Die... They Haunt You
Lessons from a Millionaire Entrepreneur

Heidi Easley

Published by Game Changer Publishing
Cover Design: Skylar Cawley

Paperback ISBN: 978-1-962656-93-1
Hardcover ISBN: 978-1-962656-94-8
Digital: ISBN: 978-1-962656-95-5

www.GameChangerPublishing.com

DEDICATION

To Bobby and Pixie, without y'all, what's the point of dreaming?

Read This First

Thank you for buying and reading my book. Please scan the QR code below to receive free gifts to help you Think Like a Creative Money Maker and more!

Simply Scan the QR Code Here:

Your Dreams Don't Die... They Haunt You

Lessons from a Millionaire Entrepreneur

Heidi Easley

www.GameChangerPublishing.com

Praises for Heidi

"Courageous! That's how I see Heidi Easley and her beautiful family. Heidi and her family have overcome so many painful obstacles that life has thrown at them and have persevered with their love of each other, family, friends, and God—not necessarily in that order. Through all her pain, heartbreak, and loss, Heidi has maintained her contagious smile and 'can do' attitude. This has given her the strength to move forward and become a loving wife, mother, and woman of God. She has become a very successful artist and businesswoman and has encouraged all those who know her that they too can overcome life's difficulties if they have the love and encouragement from those closest to them."

- Rosemary Reynolds, Helping Artist Coordinator/Creative Marketing Coordinator DecoArt, Inc.

"Heidi lights up a room! I love that she has never been a gatekeeper in the industry. She gives generously, and her heart to serve is revealed within moments of talking with her. Her 'dream big' attitude is contagious and inspires me to aim higher!"

- Danielle Stringer, Founder of Imperfect Dust | Hand Lettered Art by Danielle

"Heidi is the perfect example of someone who has not only lived her own dream but inspired thousands of others to do the same. I'm so excited for this book to show others how to take massive action and live the life they were meant to live, in spite of whatever doubts, fears, or obstacles get in the way. Read this book, follow Heidi's example, take action on the lessons she shares… then read it again and again."

- Matt McWilliams, bestselling author of *Turn Your Passions Into Profits*

"Heidi is someone who motivates you to go for your dreams and go big! She not only possesses a business-savvy mind but also a heart of gold to go along with it. She truly wants others around her to succeed in all they do."

- Stacey Collins, Owner, Wilshire Collections

"Heidi is the biggest dreamer I know. She is also driven to fearlessly and rapidly take action to move towards her big dreams. This combination has brought her success after success. It has been amazing to watch her grow as an entrepreneur and leader in her field. I am so proud of her and feel lucky to witness everything she is doing firsthand. She is the love of my life!"

- Bobby Easley, Husband and Business Partner

"Heidi is someone who consistently exceeds expectations for her clients. As a compassionate, diligent, and dedicated business owner, she has achieved remarkable success over the years. Through her Texas Art and Soul paint party coaching business, she transforms the dreams of other small business owners into reality."

- Chris Triest, Key Account Manager, Constant Contact

"Heidi is a motivated, professional ray of light! Her enthusiasm and curious nature allow her to fully engage in any endeavor. Fully embracing artistic agency, she joyously leads from a heart-centered space of gratitude."

- Tracy Lee Stum, Founder of TiLT A Tracy Lee Stum Museum, www.tracyleestum.com

"There are just so many positive words I would use to describe Heidi. We came to know each other as she was on the 'upswing' from a very difficult time in her life. So, for me, she has been such a humble, hardworking, determined woman who wouldn't let anything stand in her way. Heidi is one of the best examples of a 'Ray of Sunshine,' always positive, upbeat, smiling. She is always looking for a way through when people say 'no' or 'that can't be done.' Heidi would come back with 'why not' or 'can we try this to make it work.' Knowing her and seeing what she has risen from makes me a better person because it shows me that anything can be done as long as you remain positive."

– Susan Rogers, VP of Sales, Gare Ceramics

"Imagine seeing something so clearly in your mind, and then it becomes a reality a short while later. I've watched Heidi do this in her business, inspiring thousands of others to do the same along the way. If you want more out of life, Heidi is the person to show you how to make it happen."

– Stu McLaren, Co-Founder of Searchie

"Heidi is not only one of the most creative people I know, but she is a true encourager - she believes in sisterhood by calling out those strengths you didn't know you had. In the ten-plus years I've known Heidi, she has been a friend, mentor, and someone who continues to inspire me."

– Jennifer Eikenhorst, Author and Host of *Accidental Hope Podcast*

To the Dreamer,

You are magically made, overly optimistic, and perfectly placed to bring hope to the world.

By dreaming out loud and unapologetically, you unconsciously allow others to do the same!

So keep your head in the clouds and take those risks because people need you more than you know.

You see... each soul is a piece of the grand puzzle. Without the dreamer, the world is incomplete, like a missing star from the night sky.

However, when the dreamer realizes that it's okay to choose happiness and chase irrational sparks of imagination, they're also creating a path for those yet to come.

So… Cheers to you, the magically made, the overly optimistic, and the perfectly placed.

– Heidi

Foreword

When my mom first asked me to write her a foreword, my first question was, "What the heck is a foreword?" To which she replied, "I actually don't know." So, after figuring out what a foreword is, here I am about to write one.

Over the past several years, my mom has had some pretty crazy ideas. Some involve a "Slime camp" in which kids from all over town would come and spend six hours at our house destroying our kitchen. Others were just simply adding in shopping time to the half hour we had before leaving for a flight. She always added some kind of fun adventure to everything we would do. I am so grateful that her spirit passed on to me as well.

While growing up, I saw her struggle, work, triumph, and fail again and again. Her work ethic is unmatched. No matter how many times she fell on her butt, she would get back up and try again. But she never JUST tried again; she would put in double the amount of effort and try it from a new perspective. My mom has always instilled in me that we never give up. Once we start something, we should stick it out. She was always the best example of that. Once she started her business, she didn't give up. She got close at some points, but she never did. She would just put on another motivational podcast and keep going.

I remember one time on our way to Florida, we were listening to "The Debt Free Scream" from Dave Ramsey's podcast, and we got pulled over for speeding. The cop asked her why she had been speeding, to which she told him the whole story of this family who was finally debt free. The police then went on to say that his mother LOVES that podcast and let us go with a warning. Our car rides are always filled with either Dave Ramsey or Sabrina Carpenter.

My mom has been such a role model to me and has taught me everything from life advice to business strategies. Her book, though filled with stories from my childhood, is such an inspiration. Thank you Mom, for everything that you have offered me in life, and thank you for always being the biggest inspiration in my eyes.

– *Pixie Easley*

Table of Contents

INTRODUCTION

Take a deep breath... And so it begins...

This book is kind of like a "confession of a creative mind."

You will learn lessons I wish I had known years earlier! There are takeaways and action steps at the end of each section, and I will walk you through how to take action despite fear to create the life you want.

From bankruptcy to million-dollar business owner, this book is for those wanting to DREAM BIG *and* take action. Feel free to read it cover to cover or skip around to the sections that most interest you. Grab your favorite pen and get ready to write down takeaways.

This book is for you if you're seeking happiness and a roadmap to overcome the obstacles preventing you from pursuing your desired life.

It's also for you if you're a creative person struggling to find confidence in yourself.

BANKRUPTCY TO BUSINESS OWNER BEFORE THE AGE OF 30

Yep, that's me.

I was raised with the principle that it's okay to borrow as long as you pay back your debts. My husband Bobby and I found ourselves overextended and then lost our jobs. At the time, I thought I was the only one going through bankruptcy. I felt ashamed, embarrassed, broke, and alone. I had no idea that millions of other families were going through the same thing. I remember not wanting my friends to think differently of me, so I kept my struggle a secret from them. However, when I look back, seeing how I lost my car, house, and everything else, I'm sure they knew what was going on.

Using art to heal, I started painting these little wooden surfboards I cut out at my sister's house. They were about 10 inches long and easy to carry to the school, where I taught 850 students weekly as an art teacher. During breaks or lunch, I would paint on the surfboards to escape my reality. Kids would see the surfboards on the counter and yell, "Mrs. Easley, can you paint me a surfboard? Can you put my name on it?"

I would respond, "No, these are just for fun."

However, as more and more kids saw these boards and begged for one, I had a realization after about the 150th request. I thought, *Maybe I could sell these.* I called my mother-in-law with my idea, and before I knew it, we were meeting with the head of Pier Park (shopping center) in Panama City Beach, FL. The wooden surfboards were still wet with polyurethane I had sprayed on them that morning. Holding one up, I was surprised when he said, "I think you could make a lot of money with these." We negotiated a deal to rent a 10 ft. x 10 ft. space in front of Starbucks for $1,200 a month to sell hand-painted surfboards.

I roped my whole family in. My hubby and my father-in-law were helping cut and sand the boards, and my mother-in-law and I were priming the boards and stacking them in totes. We even had my daughter Pixie painting surfboards while I worked on designs. She was only 2 but very involved, which was quite amusing. This was the first time in a while that I had felt hope. Since we were struggling financially, my mother-in-law suggested we do this on a 50/50 basis. They would cover all the expenses for supplies, rent, and help us with cutting boards, priming, and preparing for me to hand paint. Then, from the earnings, we would pay the costs and split the profit 50/50.

Finally, the day arrived to set up and sell these magnificent surfboards.

But, NO ONE IS BUYING THEM.

I'm beyond devastated. Sitting in my little booth, which we created with two 6-foot tables, makeshift tablecloths, and examples of painted surfboards all around, I felt like a complete loser again.

So, what do you do when you've lost everything before the age of 30? You go to Buffalo Wild Wings and have a drink at the bar. One drink in, and I'm thinking, *Life is hard. How can I fail this much before I'm 30? I have a little girl, and I want to give her a great life, but I can't figure out how to make enough money to support her.* Another drink in, and I'm thinking, *This sucks! This was my plan B. What am I supposed to do now?*

Then my husband calls, and everything changes.

He says, "Get over here... we have orders!"

I'm like, "No, we don't. You're lying."

He repeats, more seriously, "Get over here... we have orders."

My eyes widen, and I look at my mother-in-law. She says, "Go!"

Buffalo Wild Wings was right across the street from where we set up. I walk across the street, a bit tipsily, and my husband shows me this stack of tickets. They are all the orders that have come in. He holds them, looks at me, and says, "Get to painting."

You should have seen the smile on my face.

A moment before, I felt like I was on the ground, done for, count me out. Then it was like God scooped me up and not only said, *"It's going to be okay,"* but also, *"You are going to be able to paint for the rest of your life."*

We painted over 1,000 surfboards in just two months, earning more than $20,000. As the slowest painter ever—it used to take me a year to finish one painting—I had to work quickly. Every $20 surfboard brought us $20 closer to my family's future. Sometimes, we would receive 60 orders in one night, and I would stay up until 3 a.m. to complete orders for the next day's pickup. If it was raining, which often happens in Florida, my friend Alyson and I would paint in my car. We did everything possible to make it work.

Takeaways

- You can fail and still have a second, third, or fourth chance. In my twenties, I didn't realize that life is about learning and growing. I just thought if you screwed up, it's over. But that is far from the truth.
- My bankruptcy was one of the best things that had ever happened to us. Although it felt like torture at the time, it taught me so much about money. And it showed me that God always has my back.
- One of the biggest lessons was about timing. People were on the beach during the day and then ready to eat and shop at night. If I had given up too soon, I wouldn't have seen the awesomeness that was coming.

LET'S TAKE ACTION: Have you ever had a time in your life when you almost gave up on a dream right before it took off? Are there some things that you wish you hadn't given up on? What is one thing you can do tomorrow that ultimately moves you back on the path toward your dream?

____

____

____

____

YOU ARE MAGICALLY MADE

"I'm talking to you. Yes, YOU!" *You* are magically made.

Take that in for a minute.

Before you get too far in this book, I want you to realize how important you are and what you have to offer MATTERS! You are worthy of happiness and a life well lived! You are worthy of all that God has for you. You have a purpose.

Have you ever met someone who just radiates happiness? Their outlook on life always seems positive. You've never heard them swear. Their social media photos look perfect. There must be something wrong, right? I used to be somewhat leery of people like that, as if something was being hidden—their life couldn't be *that* good. Then I realized we ALL have things we hide. We choose what we share on social media; we act differently in front of different groups of friends, and, most importantly, we behave differently when we are alone. There is a social media version of life, and then there's the version of life happening on the down days, the normal days, and the days not worth posting about. Everyone has those days when they just want to lay in bed and not think about anything or anyone. But does that mean you're not worthy of living an amazing, busy life? Absolutely not. God cares about all the small wins, even if it happens to be making your bed that day. Your little wins are still worth something, even if you think they don't measure up to the perfection blasted on social media.

Takeaways

- Be cautious when on social media; not everything is real life.
- God cares about the small *and* large wins.

LET'S TAKE ACTION: Take a couple of minutes to think about what you've done today or in the past week that could be considered a win, whether it's something as simple as making your bed or achieving something significant in your life. Write it down in the format "I am proud of myself for _____."

___

___

___

___

THE SUCK ZONE

WHO AM I TO WANT THIS?

So you've figured out what you want and have started to take steps that lead you toward your goals. However, there is still that little voice in the back of your mind saying: *Who am I to want this,* or even more so, *who am I to DESERVE this?*

One of my favorite authors, Marianne Williamson, says:

"We ask ourselves, 'Who am I to be brilliant, gorgeous, talented, fabulous?' Actually, who are you not to be? You are a child of God. Your playing small does not serve the world. There is nothing enlightened about shrinking so that other people won't feel insecure around you. We are all meant to shine, as children do. We were born to manifest the glory of God that is within us. It's not just in some of us; it's in everyone. And as we let our own light shine, we unconsciously give other people permission to do the same. As we are liberated from our own fear, our presence automatically liberates others."

Having gone through bankruptcy at a young age, I lost my confidence and had to rediscover it. Thankfully, God picked me up and showed me He is a God of 2nd, 3rd, 4th—unlimited chances. He uses the broken, the so-called undeserving, the forgotten. He chooses YOU every time. He is for you and truly loves you.

When I first started my "cute little business," as some would call it, my family and friends were big supporters. Everyone loves an underdog. My perception and the words said to my face were usually kind. It was almost as if they took on my business as a school project. They were rooting for the kid who may not win the race but finished last. And not just last, but finished when everyone has gone home, and the track lights are turned off.

Cheering on the underdog is easy because they struggle. It makes it easy to root for them because all they have to do is better than they did last time. The problem with this is that, unfortunately, some people love to see another person struggle. It makes them feel better—more accomplished. It's as if they're thinking, *At least I'm not doing that badly.* Their self-esteem is lifted, but not yours.

You are still diligently working on your "cute business" while the world moves on and thinks this dreamer/believer phase will eventually pass. No harm done, right?

Except your self-esteem takes a hit. Your confidence takes a hit—until you start to make progress. Then, a whole different realm enters your world! It's almost as if there's an alternate universe you didn't know existed. It's like you've leveled up in Nintendo's Mario Brothers! You hit the gold coin or the mushroom, and suddenly, you see a whole different side of people and the world that you didn't know was there! Your confidence and self-esteem begin to soar. You start to feel accomplished, powerful, and on the right track. However, the downside can be family and friends start to see you differently.

Then…

You hit a roadblock, go back two steps, and feel defeated. But, lucky you, your friends and family "lift" you up. Then your confidence can take a hit because why are they only supporting me when I'm on the ground? It's a mind game.

So, what's the solution? How do you build self-confidence and self-esteem?

I have studied this for many years, witnessing it in real time in my own life and through numerous conversations with other successful entrepreneurs.

You need to become your biggest cheerleader. What does that look like?

Takeaways

- Celebrate the wins, both little and big!
- Celebrate the failures, too, because, from them, you learn what not to do next time.
- Remember not to rely on family and friends to be as excited for you as you would like them to be. I say this not out of meanness to any family and friends, but when you start to succeed, they might not share your enthusiasm.

LET'S TAKE ACTION: Put on your favorite song. One of mine is "Make Room" by The Church Will Sing. Now, write down a list of how you believe God sees you. His opinion is truly the only one that matters. Also, write down your reason for starting your business. When you feel like no one believes in you, come back to this list and reflect on why you're trying to accomplish your goals.

____

____

____

____

SNAKE TRAILER

For two and a half years, we lived in a trailer house on a river in Texas. It was the first place we "bought," or more accurately, the first for which we took out bank loans. We had such high hopes for this place: three acres on a river and a small country church down the road. This was the first time in my life I regularly attended church. It was also the first time I experienced a church split, which changed me for life. For anyone who the church has hurt, remember to put your faith in God, not people; they will fail you.

It took me more than ten years of hurt and pain to really understand that, at the end of the day, we have to put our faith in God and not people.

One of my favorite verses that I always come back to is *"Love God with all your heart, all your soul, and all your mind." (Matthew 22:37).*

Back to the snake trailer. Being on a river in Texas on newly cleared land brought snakes—lots of them. We had a couple of dogs my dad dropped off as a present, and that led to dog food in the house, which attracted mice, which in turn brought snakes coming in to eat the mice.

My first snake encounter happened after a late night in Austin. We were with my sister and brother-in-law. Coming home from a late-night mini-golf course around midnight, I rushed into the house to use the bathroom. With my pants halfway down, I looked up and saw a 5-foot snake stretched across the bathtub in front of me.

As I write this, I'm getting chills on the back of my neck. I HATE snakes!

Frozen with my pants halfway down, I pulled them up, screamed as loud as I could, and ran! I bolted out of the house, down the makeshift stairs, and locked myself in my car, crying hysterically. Bobby calmly said, "That's a snake scream."

My sister and her husband at the time went inside to find the snake. My scream scared it, so it was hidden in a tight circle behind a small mirror on the counter by the sink. It took them quite a while to get it out of the house, and we moved in with my parents for about two weeks.

Each time I encountered a snake, or a snake encountered me, we would move out for several days until I felt I could handle it. I prayed non-stop, knowing God was protecting me.

One day, I came home from work and school and wanted to start some laundry. When I opened the cabinet above the washer to get the detergent, a water moccasin struck at me! I quickly closed the cabinet and, in a frenzy, jumped around, pulling at my clothes to make sure it wasn't on me. Then, I moved back into my parents' house for several days.

Bobby and a neighbor spent over an hour fighting that one; it was mean and poisonous. We had many other snakes come through that trailer. I found a baby copperhead under the kitchen sink and rattlesnakes in the yard. Our dogs tried to fight those and would always lose, as evidenced by their swollen faces when they came home.

One afternoon, before heading to my bank job, I decided to "clean up the backyard." My plan was to pick up sticks and make a little section look pretty. As I was walking around in my bank skirt attire (what was I thinking?), I saw a snake about 3-4 feet long. I called my neighbor and grabbed the shotgun. She came over and suggested, "Let's not shoot it. Grab the shovel, and we'll chop off its head." Terrified and thinking this was not a good idea, I watched her grab the shovel. The snake was now by the picnic table my dad had made for us. My neighbor used the shovel to pin the snake's head down, but instead of killing it, it just made it angry. Very angry. She then told me to grab a tool from under the trailer. My husband had some random tools lying around, including an old pair of tree cutters. I grabbed them, and she asked me to hold the shovel while she attempted to cut off the head.

So there I was, in a skirt, standing on the picnic table, pressing a shovel against a snake's head. This was a moment when I *really* questioned my life choices. What I hadn't anticipated was the snake's tail ferociously whipping about, almost hitting me as I cried to the sky, praying for God's help.

The cutters weren't sharp, so we struggled with the snake for what felt like an eternity (probably about 20 minutes). Finally, she separated the head from the body, and the snake was dead. I reminded her we should have used the shotgun, and now I was late for work.

I proudly placed the snake's head in the BBQ pit, eager to show Bobby and share the story of the snake that stood no chance.

I became so tired from dealing with snakes and financial struggles that I told Bobby, "Let's move."

When he asked where, I replied, "Anywhere but here."

We talked about North Carolina and Florida, eventually settling on the latter. We had family who owned a trailer in Panama City Beach, FL, so we asked about renting it for a month while we looked for a permanent place. In just a month, we sold everything, convinced my sister and her husband to join us, and started fresh in Panama City Beach, FL.

Years after relocating to Florida, Bobby revealed that he had found several snake skins beneath our heated water bed while moving out. I'm immensely grateful we took action to escape a situation that seemed destined for an emergency room visit due to a poisonous snake bite.

Takeaways

- Just because you buy a house doesn't mean you are stuck there for life.
- If you need to change your situation, make the change.
- Snakes suck.

LET'S TAKE ACTION: Dolly Parton famously said, "If you don't like the road you're walking, start paving another one!" This is what we did. We needed to move. I'm not saying you need to move like we did, BUT is there something you need to change in your life?

___

___

___

___

TOSTITO CHIPS AND TIDE

During the winter, I visited my mother-in-law's house to warm up and use her washing machine after ours broke down shortly following the water moccasin incident. Our trailer couldn't retain heat and had holes from tons of mice. We had borrowed $6,000 to purchase this house, which was far from perfect.

We would activate our water bed heater, set up a space heater in the room, and close all other doors. Waking up to a freezing house, where even the dish soap in the kitchen would be frozen, I'd quickly grab what I needed and head to my mother-in-law's until work. I took showers, watched TV, did my laundry with Tide detergent, and snacked on their Tostitos chips and my father-in-law's Ensure. I remember thinking, *This is the life! One day, I'll be able to afford Tide detergent and Tostitos chips—the name brands.* To me, that was the definition of success, a sentiment that largely holds true even today.

Takeaways

- Not everyone has the same definition of success.

LET'S TAKE ACTION: Make your dream list. What would define success for you right now?

____

____

____

____

OVERNIGHT SUCCESS = LIES

One of the things I wish someone had told me is that there is really no such thing as overnight success. In today's world, it seems like everyone is winning online. Overnight, you'll be rich, have passive income, and everything you want. But it's not true. You can get pulled in a million different directions, and often it is not the right direction for you. If you see someone with success, even a little, there's a past that has led them to arrive at that moment. Usually, it's ten or more years of consistently showing up.

One of the best pieces of advice I've been given is to "under promise and over deliver." In most cases, the average person is on autopilot. If you really look at your days, are they all the same? The average person goes to work and comes home. They have a dream or an idea they want to pursue, but life gets in the way. The responsibilities of taking care of kids, providing for your family, and the occasional vacation have every penny spent and every ounce of energy zapped. However, this is what separates the average from the dreamer. The dreamer will continue pursuing the thing they love no matter what. The dreamer will know it's hard and will feel like it will never happen, but then, one day, there's an opening. One day, it feels like there's hope. Then another day happens, and two steps back. Then, the dreamer gets back up time and time again, knowing that there will be pain involved in pursuit.

When I was teaching full time and teaching paint parties several times a month, I also started my online business. I remember talking to a friend, and I asked her, "Does it have to be this hard? I want to keep doing my business, but it's not where it needs to be for me to quit my other job."

She said something that stuck with me: "Sometimes you just have to suck it up. It won't be like this forever."

That was such a powerful statement because it reminded me that I have to keep working hard if I really want it. So many times in life, we are given permission to slack off. "It's okay, give yourself grace," they say, which, believe me, I think is important. However, it's also important to work hard. If it were easy, everyone would do it. I always think of JLo in this situation. I heard an interview where she mentioned how she will outwork anyone. I have adopted that attitude. I will always outwork everyone in the room.

Another thing I wish someone had told me was that when you finally reach your dream, you'll fear losing it. There was a time when you didn't have money, and then there were times you did. It was like an on-and-off relationship. Now, you have to commit to showing up every day. Now, you're playing another game: how to maintain success. This was a wake-up call for me. I was constantly struggling. Once I finally reached a point of so-called success, another fear quickly emerged: *Who am I to have this money? Do I deserve this? Is it okay to spend? How do I manage it?* So many fears entered my mind. I often felt, and still feel, like I must pay for everyone's meal every time I go out to eat, as if it's some sort of guilt for finally making money. It was a strange feeling, eating me alive, so Bobby suggested a therapist. Again, another weird thought: being able to afford a therapist. She asked me if I would be mad, give it back, or be upset if a friend gave me a gift. Of course not. I would thank my friend for the gift. She suggested that instead of having so much fear around having money, I should take a minute to thank God for what I have. It's a gift. I'm still very new to this (20-year) overnight success, but it's very helpful to know that these are new skills we have to learn. How could I be good with money if I've never had money to manage?

Takeaways

- It's important to remember that running a successful business will take patience and time.

- Being an entrepreneur means you can't bail on your business when it gets tough; you have to stick with it and believe in yourself.
- If you want your business to be successful, you must work on it daily.

LET'S TAKE ACTION: Write down how long you have been working on your business.

____

____

____

____

TROLLS ARE A GOOD SIGN

Troll*: to make a deliberately offensive or provocative online post with the aim of upsetting someone or eliciting an angry response from them. (Merriam-Webster)*

I'd like to expand this definition to include trolls in person as well. Building the life YOU want can make others uncomfortable. When I first started building my online business, it wasn't a big deal. Not many people knew I was even taking action to build an online business, so there were no trolls. However, things changed when my consistent efforts began to attract attention. My Facebook Lives went from having only my mom watching to hundreds of people.

It took time, but eventually, my work started to get noticed—then the trolls appeared. Initially, I was shocked. How could people be so cruel, commenting on my appearance and criticizing me? It was like being on the big screen with a bunch of movie critics judging me.

I even experienced it in real life. I vividly recall a family reunion one summer, where a relative asked in a condescending tone, "Do you really think quitting your job is wise? Is your business really going to work?" Or at least, that's how I heard it in my head.

I promptly responded with, "We will soon find out," and ended the conversation.

It made me realize that their approval does not equal their permission. I neither need nor want a distant relative's opinion on what I can or cannot do, just as I don't need to grant them permission to quit their job or pursue their dream. Too often, we don't take action due to someone else's judgment. I was like that for a long time. Then I realized that we do have a say in our own lives.

So now, when I encounter a troll online or have to deal with someone in real life questioning my decisions, I take a moment to consider if their input has any merit. If it lacks merit, I don't give it another thought.

Takeaways

- As you start living your life the way you want, you will encounter trolls—online or in person, sometimes both.
- When people are mean, it's not really about you.
- Their approval does not equal their permission, nor do you need it.

LET'S TAKE ACTION: Write down three things that no one can take from you, whether that's your personality, your ability to see the good in others or your favorite pair of shoes.

____

____

____

____

$15,000 LESSON

This was a hard lesson to learn, but I'm glad I did. In life and in business, you will learn hard lessons, sometimes painful to your wallet. This was one of them. I hired a firm that I thought had my best intentions, but after a month, I realized they did not. It cost $15,000 to help with my online business. They were going to create some cool stuff to help me. I was new in the online world and trusted them. Plus, they looked like a very sweet boy band, so maybe my judgment was a little cloudy. They said everything I wanted to hear and finally delivered the product. I couldn't get it to work, so I sent an email asking if they could help me with the issue I was having, which was probably a 20-minute fix. Instead, they responded with a very long email and videos explaining how they had finished their job and that if I needed anything additional, it would be more money.

They literally spent more time creating a video to outline their contract than they did fixing the issue. They didn't realize that by simply completing the job and satisfying a customer, they could have earned many referrals; instead, they showed their true colors.

I couldn't get the mistake out of my head. One day, as I was driving, I told my daughter the story, and she said, "Can you do anything about it?"

I said, "Not really."

"Then just let it go," she responded. That easy. So I did. I let it go and chalked it up to a $15,000 mistake I'll never have to learn again. It also taught me that NO ONE will care about my business the way I do. To them, it was just a job; to me, it was everything.

Takeaways

- No one will care about your business as much as you do.
- Don't let a mistake stop you from pursuing your dreams.

LET'S TAKE ACTION: Is there a mistake or lesson that you've held a grudge about? Write it down with a pencil. Now, look at it and erase it. Erase it from the page and from your mind. The problem has passed; there is nothing you can do about it now. In my daughter's words, "Let it go."

____

____

____

____

PECKED TO DEATH BY DUCKS

"It may not be okay right now, but it will be." My mom used to say that to all of us kids. She had this sign on the front porch that read, *"Raising kids is like being pecked to death by ducks."* I thought that was the best sign ever. We definitely didn't make it easy on my parents; there was always more than one of us getting into trouble. I'm sure many times, it really did feel like they were being pecked to death by ducks.

Growing up in a small town, there wasn't much to do but get into trouble. One Friday night, before the football game, I decided it was a great idea to get drunk before showing up. As a twirler, I had to perform for the halftime show and on the sidelines throughout the game. Apparently, I wasn't as smart as I thought because the superintendent pulled me off the field—I was in pretty big trouble. The town was so small that my parents knew about it before I was even off the field.

Another time, I drank beer with some friends and a senior (we thought he was hot) during lunch. When we returned to school, we were suspended within minutes and put in "in-school suspension" until our parents could pick us up. My parents would ground me for weeks; once, they grounded me for an entire summer.

My parents always wanted the best for us; they wanted to protect us. As we got older, our problems got bigger than getting drunk on a football field. What I love so much is that my mom would always say, "It's going to be okay." Those few words still make me realize today that it will be. There will be times when life sucks and kicks you in the stomach, even bringing you to your knees. But it will always get better, and eventually, it will be okay.

Takeaways

- It's going to be okay.
- Sometimes life sucks, but it will get better.

LET'S TAKE ACTION: What is a phrase that sticks with you? A phrase that reassures you that you will get through this, that this time shall pass.

____

____

____

____

DON'T LOSE YOURSELF

Years ago, Bobby and I worked with some friends at Nextel during our corporate days. Imagine a boring-looking building with key cards to get in and cubicles everywhere, as far as you could see. Hundreds of people worked at this call center, one of the highest-paying jobs without a degree in the area. Bobby and I both got jobs there, and this is where we met several friends, including "for-lifers" Alyson and Dana. The days at the call center were long but fun! Imagine a scenario just like the hit TV show *The Office,* with all the shenanigans. It was similar. Bobby was a team leader, and I was in Workforce Management, a fancy title for "boring."

One day, my friend Alyson and I saran-wrapped one of our coworker's cubicles. She couldn't even get inside to work. It was hilarious. Another time, we came to work early and put Post-it notes all over the entire desk area. There was always some kind of trouble we were trying to get into, or at least make it to where we weren't bored to death.

While working there, we were given stock options. So, anytime Bobby and I were short on money or wanted something fun, we would cash out stock options. It was a quick click of a button, and within a few days, we would have a couple of grand in our bank account. We were definitely NOT mature enough for this at this stage of our lives.

Spending five years in cubicle hell, I learned so much. But I also learned that this was not where I belonged. Maybe it was where I belonged for a short season, but it was not meant to be forever.

During my time there, I often traveled to Las Vegas for business trips. Flying from Florida to Las Vegas was a full day. There was ALWAYS a layover and delay in Atlanta. You never had a non-stop flight, so you always had to be ready for the long haul. The Vegas trips were always fun and exciting, but I was so broke! If we cashed out stocks, we would have it spent within two days. Las Vegas trips were reimbursed, but I had to have the money to pay for my own food, entertainment, etc. When it was possible, I tried going to lunch with someone or tagging along with a group so they would pay for my meal.

On one trip, I had only $60 to my name for the entire four days. The company paid for the DoubleTree Hotel, so I always knew I would have cookies that I could eat for free. Again, was this plain old resourcefulness or just flat-out stupidity? I'm not really sure which one. Anyway, I say don't lose yourself because I was on a corporate path doing something I hated. I was in charge of spreadsheets, call volume, and endless meetings with supervisors pretending to know what was going on. I also remember supervisors falling asleep during meetings. But I was in it! I was climbing the corporate ladder—until I wasn't.

The day came when I thought I was going to be told I had a promotion. That sentence alone drives me nuts. I don't like the feeling of waiting for someone else to decide the fate of MY life. Anyway, I was called into the big boss's office, thinking she was about to tell me that I had been promoted. But that's not what happened. She told me they gave MY promotion to another guy who worked in another department. Of course, I would still stay in my position and do the same amount of work, but now he would be my supervisor, and I would answer to him. I was also asked if I could teach him everything he needed to know to take the role. As she broke this news to me, I stood in her office, trying to hold back the tears. I spent years working my butt off, only to be passed up by someone else for the big promotion I was hoping for. I left that meeting, went back to my desk, packed up my laptop, left the building, and cried all the way home.

Once I let the dust settle, I remembered how I had always wanted to be an art teacher. I wasn't made for numbers and spreadsheets. My soul actually craved being around paint and creating. So, out of anger, I got back to pursuing what I really wanted in life: to teach art. Within a year, I left Nextel, and shortly afterward, I landed a job teaching art at a middle school. Life was back on track, or so I thought.

Takeaways

- Don't get stuck at a job for the wrong reasons.
- True happiness can be found when you are doing something you love.

LET'S TAKE ACTION: Were you stuck at a job you didn't like? What made you decide to leave it? Are you on a completely different path from where you wanted to be? What small step can you take this week to help you find yourself again?

____

____

____

____

OVERWHELMING PURPOSE

This will NOT happen at first! When I first started a side gig, I was just trying to make extra money. After many years, I felt like my purpose had found me. Since I was 14, my dream has been to be an art teacher. In elementary school, my art teacher had us create giant paper mache dinosaurs to be put on the stage in the cafeteria. It was a huge project, and she would have students work after school on it. I LOVED this project! I loved the feeling of something so cool coming together and being a part of a project that was bigger than just myself.

Fast forward years later, and I finally became an art teacher myself. I created BIG projects that the students could get involved with, whether it was school-wide murals, massive full-day chalk art festivals, or even family art nights. I always wanted to make sure kids had art to feel like they had a purpose.

After teaching for many years, I kept being pulled into my business stuff. I loved having a side gig that helped my family make extra money. It also excited me that I could come up with something, make it happen, and then see a financial benefit.

One day, I was finishing up art club with the 5th-grade students. I had the perfect school district, the perfect art classroom (with a window), and the perfect principal who trusted me and let me pursue all the giant, crazy projects with the kids. I felt so guilty for wanting to go full-time in my business, which was teaching paint parties. I felt like I had prayed for this dream, and here I was living it. How dare I want more. Then, as I was telling the kids to have a good day, standing in the doorway of my classroom, I felt like God told me it was okay to pursue my other dream. It was like I was able to dream something different.

We have several chapters or seasons in our lives, and we also have several dreams that we can fulfill. I never really stopped teaching; I just started teaching in a different way. This is when I realized *dreams don't die... they haunt you.* You can only push them back for so long, but they will always resurface. Although taking action on your dreams is terrifying, the alternative of not knowing what could have been is even worse.

Not knowing is unbearable: true potential held captive, hopes undiscovered, dreams never unlocked. My advice is to pursue every dream, even if it means pursuing what you truly love on nights and weekends. Pursue it in your spare time.

Takeaways

- Pursue every dream, even if it's only during your spare time.
- Dreams don't die... they haunt you.

LET'S TAKE ACTION: Take a minute to scribble in this section and write down what lights you up. What makes you excited to get up in the morning? (Besides knowing coffee is close by.)

____

____

____

____

BUT I DON'T HAVE TIME

"But I don't have time," says everyone in the history of everywhere. No one has time; we are all overwhelmed, overworked, and overcommitted. However, you can choose how you want to spend the little time you have. Sometimes that means saying no. Sometimes, it means choosing a different path during a particular time in your life.

I remember when I first started working as a full-time teacher. I had a new baby and was teaching paint parties on the side. I was always exhausted. Then, I felt guilty for not volunteering at the church. One day, my aunt said that teaching was a service. What I did as a teacher was giving so much of myself. I had never looked at it like that; I just saw it as a job. When I heard her say that, it made me realize that *it's okay*. It's okay that I'm not watching kids in the nursery at this time in my life. During the week, I was teaching 850 kids. My life was overwhelmed with kids. So, I spent my time helping with the art program at the church. I painted murals (my favorite) and painted live during church services.

Always make sure you are willing and able to change your goals, dreams, schedule, etc., as needed. What your life looks like right now will not be the same in a year, five years, or ten years from now.

Takeaways

- Be clear about your goals.
- Be willing to change.
- Small changes can make a big difference in your life over time.

LET'S TAKE ACTION: List your top three goals for the next year. These could include traveling with family, paying off a loan, or spending weekends on your boat. It's your choice, and there's no judgment. Being clear about your goals is important. Then, you can decide what else fits into your life. For instance, if volunteering at a local dog shelter makes you happy but you feel too busy, why not try doing it just once a month? Or commit for just one month initially? Changes don't always have to be big. Small additions here and there can still significantly enhance your life.

____

____

____

____

CRYING IN THE BATHROOM

One day, I organized a large paint party for 127 people at a church outside of Houston. It was one of my biggest paint parties, and I was terrified. I was not only expected to teach the party but also asked to share my testimony. Sharing something so personal in front of so many people had my nerves shot.

When I was in college, I had to take a public speaking class. The assignment was to write and perform an informative speech in front of my peers. I was so terrified that I used my artsy skills to create a giant paper mache Jack in the Box head to cover my face while I spoke. I even dressed up in a suit and tie, carrying a briefcase to complete the look. I felt like the Grinch when he tried to shave and put the paper bag over his head in class. My paper shook in my hands because of how nervous I was.

As I finished the speech, I felt so relieved, but the fear of public speaking still followed me all the way to this church. My parents and about five helpers were there for support. Before the event started, I went to the bathroom, overwhelmed with nerves, and began to cry. I wished I had my paper mache Jack in the box head to hide my fear. As I stood looking at my tears in the mirror, I realized this opportunity wasn't about me. I transformed my tears into a moment of gratitude. I prayed, thanking God for the opportunity and asking for the strength to focus on the participants rather than on myself. This was about them, not me. When I left the bathroom, I was on a mission to spread God's love through art, asking myself, *How can I help THEM?* The night was so much more fun as I focused on others instead of my own fears. My nerves settled the moment I began taking action.

Often, we imagine countless potential scenarios in our heads, most of which will never occur. Our brains can't always distinguish between these imagined scenarios and reality, leading to unnecessary stress. Before we know it, we're overwhelmed with fears before even starting the task at hand. In reality, those thoughts are wasted energy.

Takeaways

- Making our thoughts about gratitude vs. fear helps us overcome scary situations.
- Public speaking still sucks.

LET'S TAKE ACTION: What situation have you had in the past that you made about YOU? What is an upcoming situation where you can intentionally shine a light on the other person?

____

____

____

____

GUILT

Guilt: *feelings of deserving blame, especially for imagined offenses or from a sense of inadequacy. (Merriam-Webster)*

Social pressures define guilt differently: it's about being the perfect mom, husband, daughter, wife, sister, brother, son, friend, and so on. The list is endless. Many people are burdened by guilt, whether it's self-imposed, societal, or inherited from previous generations. For example, I have a family member who feels obligated to inform any relatives within a 12-hour radius whenever they have plans to be in the area.

Before I decided to live without guilt, it felt like a heavy blanket dampening my life, my plans, my goals, and my dreams. Have you ever had someone compliment your outfit, only for you to quickly give them a rundown of how much it cost? Not in an expensive way, but like, "I got this at Goodwill for $2," or "These jeans were on sale for only $12!" Sometimes, I would intentionally feel like I needed to justify a purchase, as if the world needs to know or even cares when or why I buy something. Guilt does WEIRD things to a brain. However, there is a better way to live: without guilt. But how? I'm glad you asked! :)

There was a time in my life when I set the boundaries, drew the line in the sand, and said no more. What this looked like for me was a time when someone I loved SO much hurt me SO badly. When this happened, I felt like my heart had been crushed. How could I disappoint someone I loved so much when I felt like I was doing the right thing?

After almost a year of therapy and lots of sadness, I learned that I had to set boundaries. This was a cycle of guilt that had happened my entire life; I decided to stop, and our relationship changed. I was still sad, but the guilt was gone. I let it go. I gave it to God. I didn't have to carry it anymore. Did the change happen overnight? No, but the strange thing was, once I decided not to let guilt control me, it was as if a fog had lifted. This might also manifest as "people pleasing." I consider myself a "recovering people pleaser." For many years, my life revolved around doing things to please others, which cost me countless hours, weeks, months, and possibly years, all spent on what OTHERS wanted. And for what? Just to not hurt their feelings?

Do you have an area in your life where you feel guilt? Can you figure out where it's coming from? Is it a feeling that makes you a little nauseous and maybe even frustrated when you think about it? Can you identify if it's a specific person or family member that you feel this guilt with? Is something causing you to not go above and beyond or holding you back because of this guilt? If you didn't have this guilt—didn't want to "people please"—what could you do in the world? Would this approach free up time both mentally and in your calendar?

We have 52 weekends in a year and only three months of summer. If you spend most of that time doing what OTHER people have planned for you, what are you truly living for?

Takeaways

- Don't spend your time doing what other people have planned for you (unless you want to).
- You have the power to let go of guilt.

LET'S TAKE ACTION: What do you want? As the Spice Girls would say, what do you "REALLY, REALLY want?"

____

____

____

____

LET'S TAKE A BREAK AND DO SOME DREAMING

Let's DREAM! Financials and logistics are NOT involved. You are just dreaming!

This leads me to a song my oldest brother shared. When I first listened, I cried. It's called 'A Symptom of Being Human' by Shinedown.

Sometimes, I'm in a room where I don't belong,
And the house is on fire, and there's no alarm.
And the walls are melting too,
How about you?
I've never been the favorite, though I'd seen it all,
Till I got my invitation to the lunatic ball.
And my friends are coming too,
How about you?
Don't worry; it's all just a symptom of being human.

As artists, creatives, and especially entrepreneurs, we often feel like we don't belong. I want to honor that.

Think of an age when you were young. For me, this age is 10.

When I was in 5th grade, I had buck teeth and literally NO friends! I remember the ONE girl who would hang out with me on the playground would punch me. I had no confidence and was so shy. My 5th-grade teacher offered to let us stay after school and read. We could bring snacks and get points to earn prizes for reading. I had the biggest crush on her nephew, so I asked my parents if I could stay and read. I still remember sitting TOTALLY silent as I ate a few snacks and read for the 30 minutes or whatever it was during that time. I was SO nervous, totally terrified, and felt VERY alone. Here's my example:

"Dear 10-year-old Heidi,

Guess what! Some really cool stuff happens! You're going to actually HOST a Painted Prom for Paint Party Business LIVE!!!! And people will want to come! Like hundreds!!!! You marry the hottest guy in school, and you have this really cool 'mini-me' daughter who will steal all your clothes and jewelry, even though she pretends she doesn't like them at first! You go on adventures, you pray together, you cry together, you laugh together! You seek oceans all across the world just to compare what it feels like to swim in different types of water. You are a self-proclaimed mermaid and spend your days swimming and painting! SO much happens! You'll lose everything and rebuild. And you will be okay! You'll have moments of extreme sadness, but also moments of extreme happiness! You have family and friends who support you even when you feel crazy! You have family and friends who will support your craziest of dreams!

So, I know you feel alone right now, but the decades ahead are pretty epic. Don't close your eyes for one second! Take it all in! Even the hard lessons!

PS: You're going to become a surfer!"

To discover what you want, I encourage you to utilize some of the DREAMING skills from the example and apply them to the following step. Write a letter to your younger self: (Bonus Points if you have a photo of yourself when you were younger to look at while you write) Spend about 10 minutes on this activity, or longer if you wish.

Takeaways

- Dream.
- Dream Big.
- Dream Often.

LET'S TAKE ACTION: It's your turn to write a letter to your younger self:

Start with - *"Dear (age) Year Old (Name),*

I recommend these two songs while writing. "A Symptom Of Being Human" by Shinedown and "Make Room" by The Church Will Sing.

____

____

____

____

____

LET'S TAKE ACTION: Now, let's write a letter to our FUTURE self! What we want, our goals, our dreams, our biggest prayers!!! This is NOT an exercise on how; it's just on WHAT you want out of life!!!! So, OVER DREAM!!!! Don't be practical! Actually, write down what you want, no matter how crazy it seems.

Example:

"Dear Future Heidi,

My hopes and dreams are big. I am living life to the fullest. I have Bobby, who loves me so much. Watching Pixie live her life and cheering her on is one of my favorite things. I have a paid-off house, travel whenever I want, and help people all over the world with ART. I have plenty and share even more! I see life as an adventure full of fun and hope. I have a second home near Zion National Park that I visit yearly. My days are filled with being inspired and contributing to others' success. I know that God put me here for a purpose.

I have a bright, fun future ahead. I can't wait until I make it all happen! And I especially can't wait to see all the surprises God has in store for me!

- Heidi"

Or Bullet Point it!

- House Paid Off
- Traveling the World
- Helping Pixie with her dreams
- Home near Zion with Bobby
- Drinking coffee every morning with a cool view!
- Contributing using God-given gifts

LET'S TAKE ACTION: Take about 10 minutes to write to your future self.

Start with - *"Dear future (Name),*

Here are two Songs I recommend playing while you write. "Crystal" by Stevie Nicks and "God Only Knows" by King and Country

____

____

____

____

____

Always remember, if you are defining your success by comparing it to someone else's success, YOU ARE ALREADY LOSING! What do YOU want!?

MARK CUBAN AND SHARK TANK

Do you watch the TV show *Shark Tank*? It debuted in August 2009, and as of the writing of this book, it's still going strong—I watch it all the time. It's one of my favorite shows because I feel like I'm being productive while relaxing. I take business notes and often order the products.

One night, I was reading Mark Cuban's book, and he had his email address in it! He mentioned in the book to email him if you had questions or perhaps business ideas—I don't remember the exact words, but I immediately emailed him, pitching an idea for doing a paint party for the Mavericks. I offered a few options and, admittedly, sent WAY too much information in that first email. However, within 20 minutes, he responded with, *"Thanks for the offer. You would be shocked at how many artists make us generous offers. Try me back in the off-season, and we can take a look."* This was back in 2013; I doubt he would email me back now.

However, those two sentences created so much hope. I have a friend, Brendin, who works for me and is great at many things. We used to teach together, and she also does photography. I taught her about the paint party business, and she took photos for me. We had a cool trade going on. So, when Mark Cuban emailed me back, it lit a fire under me. I had Brendin come and take brand-new photos at one of my paint parties, and I had my entire website redone. I wanted to be ready for the "off-season" so I could email Mark back, hoping he would want to hire me.

Well, my website was redone, and I emailed Mark a few more times but got no response. I still randomly email him every few years to see if he will reply, but I'm pretty sure he doesn't use that email anymore. This has been an ongoing theme of mine. I've reached out to Josh Gates, Kim Kardashian, and even President George Bush in the hopes of a fun collaboration.

Sometimes, the mere hope of something happening is all we need to take action. The idea of doing a paint party for someone from *Shark Tank* energized me, and the possibilities felt endless. So what if he didn't email me back. I still got my website done and lots of great photos from my friend!

Takeaways

- Never underestimate the power of hope.
- Persistence can pay off.
- Don't be scared of someone saying no.

LET'S TAKE ACTION: If you don't have Mark Cuban emailing you, create the hope yourself. What is an idea you have that would make a DREAM come true? Maybe it's a collaboration with someone. Write it down. Then, take action and contact them.

____

____

____

____

"THE ESCAPE METHOD"

I remember thinking that life would never be the same. I was right. My priorities changed. My outlook on life and family changed. Even the way I looked at my body weight changed. But what didn't change was my desire to teach people how art can heal. You see, even when I was going through dozens of heart tests, enduring many needle sticks (so many that I don't even care anymore), and having a metal parachute thingy placed in my heart, my desire to teach people how to escape their pain was still there.

I used art to heal, even through my surgery. I still held dozens of paint parties while I was healing, always with a smile on my face as I created with people. I realized that there is always something going on in everyone's life. We all have a story.

Something is going on in your life RIGHT NOW that is making you hesitant to go after the life you want, even though your soul is shouting, "*YES, I'M READY!!!*" I'm here to tell you that, even through all of my TIAs (mini-strokes), vision loss, and heart surgery, I am so thankful for my paint party escapes!

I know this sounds weird, but when I'm at a paint party helping others, my mind is TOTALLY focused on them, not on what I'm going through.

It is always like a little mental vacation for me.

I stopped thinking about the tests.

I stopped thinking about the outcome.

I stopped thinking about what might happen to me or my family.

I stopped thinking about all the dangers and risks of the surgery.

I just painted. And helped other people paint.

Please hear me when I say this: Art heals. Paint parties heal. When I took action through fear, I not only made money, but I also stayed busy and gave myself a break from thinking about all my medical troubles. *Win-win!*

Takeaways

- Art heals.
- Serving others can get your mind off of hard things.

LET'S TAKE ACTION: What in your life helps you escape when things get tough?

____

____

____

____

THEY SAID IT WAS MINOR

They say I'm being wheeled in for a minor heart procedure. They say I'm only supposed to be in there for about 30 minutes. They say I should get to go home that evening. I'm fully awake and the only one at the party with no pants on—I'm beyond freaked out. There are four sweet nurses wearing face masks, lifting me onto the slab where they will insert a catheter into my groin to plug a hole in my heart. I know, it's weird and also very impressive, considering our medical advances. Nervously, I ask the nurses around me which one will administer the drugs to help me forget this scary room. A nice lady says she shares the same birthday with me, and we chat for a moment about how nice summer birthdays are because you get presents every six months.

I again ask where the drugs are.

I'm freaking out, freezing as my legs shake and my arms have to be held up by armrests because the slab is so thin. It's the first time I've really thought about dying.

Now, I know you probably think I'm being dramatic. Remember, I'm an artist. I am ALWAYS creating things in my head. You know, like in *Alice in Wonderland,* where she talks about imagining ten impossible things before breakfast? Well, that's me in a nutshell. And I have a touch of ADHD. (My husband says it's WAY more than a touch.) My brain is going crazy. I'm flat, lying on a cold slab, totally AWARE of all my surroundings, and all I can think about is, *What if this is it? What if something goes wrong?*

The nurse next to me asks, "Are you ok?"

I tell her I'm freaking out.

She asks, "Well, did you pray?"

I reply that I did, and about a thousand other people are praying too!

I then mention that if things start to go south, please feel free to pray! I am all for it!

A few minutes later, the drug lady comes in. I am so happy to see her. She administers something in my IV, and I start to calm down. Throughout the procedure, I was in and out, but when I was awake, I remember seeing the screen the doctor was looking at and my heart beating.

I can hear them talking, and then I see something like an explosion go to the other side of my heart.

At that moment, I think the worst: *Oh no, here comes open heart surgery.* In my drug-induced haze, I yell out to the doctor, "Is everything okay??? Did it work???"

The doctor responds, "Yes, we just got it in place, now for the easy part!"

I'm awake as I hear the doctor say, "That was a difficult case, but we were successful. Good job, everyone!"

Then I hear clapping! All the doctors and nurses are clapping in the operating room.

I was the first person in Texas to have this new device installed in my heart for smaller PFOs (aka, a small hole in the heart). They say I wasn't a guinea pig; it's been tested, but the FDA had just approved it for smaller holes a few weeks before my surgery.

As I'm wheeled back into the room with my family, I have uncontrollable tears streaming down my face. I'm totally drugged up, but I know what has just happened: they closed it.

Then, the doctor comes in and tells me what a miracle it was. He says that he tried for about 5 minutes, then the doctor who did the very first PFO closure in 2003 tried for about 40 minutes until he had to leave for another surgery. It wasn't working. But a nurse, an angel named DeDe (the one who shares the same birthday as me), suggested another way to try to get the device in place, and my doctor tried one more time, this time with success!!! The doctor told my family it was by the Grace of God that it worked! The 20-minute procedure took over an hour, but it WORKED!

I went for a follow-up to see the new device in my heart and did another test, which showed that the hole was closed! I asked if Nurse DeDe was there so I could thank her in person, but she was in surgery, so I left her a message: *"This is Heidi Easley, and you were in the operating room when you did the heart procedure last week. I just wanted to thank..."* I burst out in tears as I tried to thank this lady who shared my birthday. I could barely talk as I explained how much her suggestion meant to me and how it could have possibly changed my life forever. The other sweet nurses heard me leaving the message, and we all cried. I had no idea I would burst into tears, but I think I did because I was so grateful.

Grateful for a whole heart.

Grateful for earth angels like DeDe.

Grateful for such a loving husband and family.

Grateful that the past three months of constant doctors and endless hospital bills were ending.

Grateful that I don't have to "stroke out" again.

Grateful for my next chapter.

I came home optimistic. I shared the news with my family and thought about my future. I thought about my family's future.

We all have stories. Even if you don't think you have a story, you do. Our lives are many, many chapters of hope, despair, happiness, grief, excitement, disappointments, and everything in between. If you've lived longer than a few years, you know that none of us are exempt from the awe and wonderment of life, no matter how hard it can get.

I believe our stories are meant to be shared, not only for entertainment purposes, like when you're having a glass of wine with girlfriends and share an embarrassing story, or when you need to share a hardship and need someone to listen. Our stories are meant to be shared to help others.

Takeaways

- Always be grateful.
- Surgeries are never minor.
- No one is exempt from the hardships of life, but we all choose how we handle them.
- We all have a story.

LET'S TAKE ACTION: Maybe you don't have a story about heart surgery, but you do have a story! We all do. What have you gone through and emerged as a stronger person on the other side?

____

____

____

____

THE ADVENTURE ZONE

PINK AND THE TRANSPORTER

A few weeks after my heart surgery, I attended my little cousin's wedding! His family had joined us for part of our honeymoon when he was a boy, so I thought it fitting that we attend his nuptials and playfully tease him about crashing his honeymoon.

This wedding was SO awesome! Held at The White House Mansion in Oklahoma, it felt like I was in a Hallmark Christmas movie, which, I can tell you, is my dream! Every room was adorned with Christmas decorations. After the ceremony, the dancing began. My cousin Jennifer (the groom's mother) and her cousin from New York were the shining stars on the dance floor.

As Bobby and I danced, we spotted another couple who resembled Pink, the amazing singer, and the actor from *The Transporter* movie (Jason Statham). They were incredibly cool and edgy! "Pink" was wearing a cute skirt with really high heels, and her hair, shaved on both sides, was a striking white blonde, styled high on top. "The Transporter" guy, dapper in his suspenders and bowtie, exuded a vibe suggesting that at any moment, he might need to leap into action and save the world single-handedly.

They danced their butts off the entire night, and the fact that I felt like I was hanging out with Pink was icing on the wedding cake! "The Transporter" guy was spinning her around, and they looked like kids having the time of their lives.

Finally, some country music comes on, and Bobby and I hit the dance floor. The last time we danced like this was in Nashville, TN, outside the bar Tootsies, as a street performer made up a song for us. (That's another fun story for another day.)

As we danced, we both kept an eye on "Pink" and "The Transporter" to see what they were doing, wondering what moves they had that we could copy. They were way out of our league, so we continued with our spins and the two-step we'd been doing since we were teens. I leaned into Bobby, asking him to dance with me by the Christmas tree so I could fully take in this entire Hallmark moment.

Then, we secretly watched what "Pink" and "The Transporter" were doing so we could copy them. I said, "He's dipping her!" so Bobby quickly dipped me.

"She's kicking out her legs. Wait, I don't think I can do that in these boots." Again, back to the two-step. This little spy game continued for a few songs as we tried to add new moves to our traditional two-step routine.

After a fun night of celebrating, it was time to leave. As we walked out of the party, there stood "Pink" and "The Transporter." He complimented my husband on how well we had been dancing! What??? I mean, I've won a dance-off or two in my time, but I wouldn't have said we were "good" dancers! We each complimented each other on our moves, and as we got into the car, Bobby and I felt like the cool kids in class. "Pink" and "The Transporter" liked our moves! We left feeling confident and ready to uplevel our skills at the next get-together!

Now, I know this doesn't have much to do with art, but it has everything to do with not being afraid to look foolish! There was also another guy at the wedding who looked like Ryan Reynolds (I know, a celebrity-filled wedding). He was on his cell phone the entire time. I would have pulled him onto the dance floor if I weren't married because he looked so bored. I'm not sure of his story or why he wouldn't dance. I'm also 100% certain that he thought we looked like idiots. But my point is this: always dance! Life is TOO SHORT NOT TO!!! Who cares what you look like. When you have the chance to dance, always, always dance!

Takeaways

- Dance like nobody's watching.
- Always go to weddings.

LET'S TAKE ACTION: Time to take a break! Dance for 1 minute as if no one is watching! I recommend playing "Dancing Queen" by ABBA. (It's one of Pixie's and my favorites!)

___

___

___

___

THAT TIME I HIRED BRITNEY SPEARS

I organized an event at the Gaylord Hotel in Grapevine, TX. While dining, we noticed several Britney Spears look-alikes in the hotel. Driven by curiosity, I inquired about what was happening. To our surprise, we learned that The Toxic Experience was at the hotel! The Toxic Experience is a fantastic tribute band specializing in Britney Spears covers. I'm beyond excited!

My friend Gretchen and I hurried to our room to braid our hair and dress up cutely for the Britney show. Our friends joined us, and we had a blast dancing and acting silly. That night, I discussed with Gretchen how amazing it would be to hire a Britney look-alike for our next big event. I immediately googled and messaged a Britney look-alike. For the next hour, we excitedly talked about taking dance lessons and starting our own "Toxic Experience." By the next morning, I had received a quote for hiring her, and it was affordable!

Fast forward to our big annual event. This is a massive gathering where I invite all my Paint Party Headquarters Members to meet in person. It's three days filled with business and fun. My mom described Paint Party Business LIVE as a mix between Woodstock and an old Church Revival, which I think is the perfect description. For this Paint Party Business LIVE, I had teased everyone about a surprise. I requested the family-friendly version of Britney. She was amazing! She looked and sounded just like Britney, and her backup dancers were on point. However, as I danced, I realized not everyone shared my excitement. Some people left the dance floor; others left the room entirely. During a costume change, it appeared slightly like a striptease, which was a bit cringe-worthy, but I decided to dance and enjoy the moment. Despite not everyone being on board with Britney, I wanted to demonstrate confidence in teaching and stage presence, which she indeed had. As I lay in bed that weekend, reflecting on the good and bad, I reminded myself that when I'm 88, I'll look back on this and laugh, glad I didn't take life too seriously. Did I misread the room? Yes, but was it worth it? Absolutely!

Takeaways

- Take risks because life is too short to take it too seriously.
- Find a friend like Gretchen, who will wear pigtails at a moment's notice, and when you get the chance to hire a Britney look-alike, learn all her songs and dance the night away.

LET'S TAKE ACTION: What's something you've always wanted to try but never have? When you are 88, will you look back on your life and wish you had taken more risks?

____

____

____

____

LIVING ON THE EDGE

My mother-in-law once told me I always worked teetering off the edge. I wasn't always like that. A consistent paycheck was so important to me in the past. I used to think people who didn't have a consistent paycheck were crazy. How could they sleep at night, not knowing what was coming in? One summer, I took Pixie from Texas to Florida. We were going to teach paint parties and make some money while having an adventure. Leaving Texas with all our paint party supplies and the open road ahead of us was the coolest feeling. Yes, it was a little scary, but also really fun. We would drive from Texas to South Florida, stopping along the way to see family and friends, sleeping on their couches, and eating food from their fridges.

That first summer, I only had enough money to make it to Florida, but I knew I would have a paycheck from the paint party once I got there. Looking back, it was totally irresponsible, but there was a fire inside me that craved adventure and excitement more than stability. My mother-in-law later said, "I know now you are a planner, but in the early days, you just acted."

It was so true. I just acted. I liked the feeling of moving forward. Sitting still wasn't getting me anywhere, so I acted.

Takeaways

- Sitting still won't get you where you want to be.
- Take action.

LET'S TAKE ACTION: What is something that scares you a little but you know you need to do to move forward?

____

____

____

____

THAT TIME I DID 'SHROOMS

My husband Bobby was so jealous. He had always wanted to try 'shrooms, having listened to Joe Rogan and watched numerous documentaries about their benefits. However, I needed a babysitter, so he decided to take care of me instead of partaking. Thanks, Bobby! I had been drinking wine most of the day, so when the 'shrooms showed up, I added them to the mix. That was not a good choice. I immediately became a sobbing mess, upset with myself for taking them and unable to stop crying. Bobby said, "You've done it, so now just enjoy the ride. Think of it from an artist's perspective. Look around. What do you see?" The entire sky was pixels. I felt like I was in a cartoon. I have to admit, it was pretty epic.

Here's the thing you may or may not know about 'shrooms: they're a commitment, like a 4 to 6-hour commitment. Usually, when I drink wine, I can slow down and be okay. I can sleep off a buzz. This was not that way. Every few minutes, I would come out of a trip, look at Bobby, and ask, "Is this over? When will it end?" Right behind him was a tree. This tree was alive, moving, dancing. I loved this tree. I would just look at it and cry. I think that's why I still love trees to this day. Many things happened that night, but the most profound was the sky. I looked up, and the entire sky resembled *Starry Night,* the painting, with a giant hand coming down. I prayed for God to forgive me for doing 'shrooms. I felt so ashamed, but as I looked at the sky with thousands of stars, I had an overwhelming feeling of forgiveness. God doesn't just love me when I'm good. He loves me all the time. It also gave me so much grace and forgiveness for others in my life who struggle with addictions. As I looked at the sky with tears streaming down my face, I felt God's presence. I know for sure God loves me in all situations. So, as you read this and perhaps feel a little judgy toward me, I understand. We are not perfect. We are going to have moments where we can't believe someone did that or even moments like I had where I couldn't believe I did something like that. The next day, I asked Bobby what the sky looked like, and he said it was hazy and you couldn't even see the moon. God can use any situation for His good.

Takeaways

- God loves you always.
- Forgiveness is for everyone.

LET'S TAKE ACTION: What is something you are ashamed of that you can let go of, learn from, and use to help someone else?

___

___

___

___

WE BOUGHT A ZOO

We bought a zoo! Wait, I mean a house, not a zoo!!! After losing everything, it took us a LONG time to buy a house. This was a BIG DEAL for us!!!

For eight months, amidst all the trials, we prayed for the right house to appear. We started discussing renting a larger place to store all my art supplies. My art business was taking over every room in our small house. I'm always thankful at night when I pray, but I wasn't always grateful during the day. Instead of being upset about not having enough space, I started mentally acknowledging all the things I loved about this little house. I became grateful for the garage that housed hundreds of paintings and canvases. I appreciated the fenced yard, perfect for our dog Blue to run around without wandering off on his own adventures (he was an adventurer, too!). I also started being thankful for having a space, a roof over my head, and a husband who, despite hating glitter passionately, has tolerated all of my art mess as my business grew. I felt grateful that Pixie has two closets in her room, a luxury for most girls! I began to appreciate our proximity to the school and how much gas I saved from not having to drive far.

Then something happened... I became more grateful for everything I loved about our house, and I became calmer. I started to feel at peace in this little home. I began writing things I was grateful for on my bathroom mirror with an expo marker to remind myself of what's important. My attitude and spirit about this little home changed. One day, while we were eating lunch, my husband was looking at potential rental houses. He found one, and as soon as he showed it to me, we both smiled. We drove to the house and sat in front of it. It was for sale, not rent.

Within 10 minutes, a sweet Realtor showed up, and we fell in love with the house. It had two living spaces, and one of the huge living areas would be perfect for my art studio! As we walked around the 3,400 square foot space (at the time, we lived in roughly 800 square feet), we were amazed by the possibilities! It had a shop for my husband, five bedrooms, and a large kitchen—a white kitchen, which I love. The garage space had been converted into a large area that my husband pointed out could be used for paint parties or kids' camps in the summer. It seemed too good to be true!

She told us the price, which was way over our budget. We said, "Thanks so much, and if the owners are ever interested in renting, please let us know." In our heads, we still felt like it was our house. About a week and a half later, I got a call from the Realtor. She said the owners wanted to work out a deal and would come down on the price quite a bit. After some negotiating, we settled on a price within our budget and found the money for the down payment! It all came together so easily that I knew it was a gift from God. After six moves in nine years, I'm so excited to finally be "settled," as much as any artist can be.

Why do I tell you all of this? Well, for the past few years, I've read hundreds of books and spent tons of money on coaching, and I've learned a lot! (Way more than I learned in college, but that's another story.) Anyway, the two most important things I've learned would be: ART HEALS and ALWAYS BE GRATEFUL!!!!

Takeaways

- Art heals.
- Always be grateful.

LET'S TAKE ACTION: What are you grateful for today? Bonus points if you set down your book for just a moment and send a quick text to someone you love. Just say something like, "*I am grateful for you! Thank you so much for being a part of my life!*" (See if they respond.)

____

____

____

____

OOPS!

Teaching part-time while running a business full-time can be overwhelming. One day, I hosted a paint party in the middle of the day. After cleaning up, I remembered I was responsible for picking up Pixie from school. She was in 3rd grade at the time. Having been non-stop teaching back-to-back parties, I completely forgot to unpack the car before pick-up. Rushing, I arrived five minutes late and realized the entire car was filled with paint party supplies, not just for one party, but several. It wasn't my proudest moment, but I asked her to squeeze in between the paint supplies and the driver's seat, standing up behind my seat. She thought it was a blast! Thankfully, at that time, we only lived a block from the school, but it was still embarrassing. She held on and laughed the whole way home.

Takeaways

- Luck favors the prepared.
- Don't feel like a complete loser when you make your kid stand in the backseat.

LET'S TAKE ACTION: When was a time you didn't prepare properly, and it caused a problem? How can you change that for the future?

____

____

____

____

VAN IN THE OCEAN

My parents are spontaneous. Or, more accurately, my dad is spontaneous. We would be at the mall on a Friday night, an hour from home. My dad would suddenly decide to drive several more hours to Galveston so we could see the ocean. We had many random road trips like this on the weekend, and I always loved the adventure of it—the unknown, like anything could happen. One night, my dad parked our 15-passenger van on the beach. We played in the ocean that night, and mosquitoes were eating us up while we slept in the van. In the middle of the night, my sister had to go to the bathroom. When she stepped outside the van, she stepped into the ocean. The tide had come up and was slowly sinking our one-ton van into the ocean. I remember being worried, but apparently not too worried, because we all went back to sleep until the sounds of helicopters above us awakened us. We eventually got the van out of the ocean while my dad teased my little brother for calling the police helicopters on us. It's a story that we often tell and laugh about. I often wonder how close we were to a different situation if a bigger storm had come in. But what's the fun in that?

Takeaways

- Don't sleep on the beach too close to the ocean.
- Always look at life as an adventure.

LET'S TAKE ACTION: What's your last big adventure? What is something fun you can do this weekend that would create a memory for you and your family?

____

____

____

____

ROAD TRIP RESOURCEFULNESS

Resourcefulness is rewarded. Before I had money, I had resources. I knew where to find every free cookie, grocery store sample, back-to-school haircut, and even the Taco Casa courtesy cup, which I still use to this day. When my daughter Pixie was little, she knew the routine: hit the bakery first for a free cookie, then go grocery shopping around lunchtime when there are endless samples and free wine tastings for me! We had a full meal by the time we finished shopping.

Resourcefulness is underrated.

When Pixie was little, I would take her to the mall. There's always a train or a carousel nearby. Since we were on a budget, I wouldn't spend the money to make the train or carousel move. Instead, I would have Pixie jump on it and play. She never knew the toy trains or carousels moved. There was a large train that would drive around the outdoor mall called Pier Park in Panama City Beach, FL. I taught her how fun it was to smile and wave at the other kids as the train went by. Until one day, her grandma ReeRee bought her a train ticket.

In my defense, she was just as happy watching the train as she was riding it. (Actually, not really—Pixie LOVED that train!) *(note added by Pixie)*

Another time, in the fall, we headed to the State Fair of Texas. It's a pretty big deal, and we were so excited to go and show our daughter Big Tex (the iconic giant statue) and eat all the fried foods. After being stuck on the transportation system for over two hours, we decided to ditch the fair. We didn't want to disappoint Pixie, so we got resourceful. On the way home, we stopped at a pizza place called Gattitown. They had great pizza, games, a few very small rides, and movies! We had a blast and pretended it was the State

Fair! Pixie was too young to know the difference. We saved a ton of money while still having a fun day!

Resourcefulness.

On one of our trips, we were kicked out of a timeshare. Let me explain. I saw a sign on the highway advertising Disney and Universal Studios tickets. Pixie and I were headed to my friend Mindy's house, and needing a break from the long drive, I decided to pull over and talk to them. I had no idea it was a timeshare trap. The guy at the counter offered a free night at a hotel and tickets to Universal Studios. Pixie was in her Harry Potter phase, and I really wanted to get those tickets. He asked if I was married (for the income requirement), and I said yes. He then suggested that since my husband wasn't with me, I should pretend to be unmarried. Against my better judgment, I told Pixie we would attend the meeting and pretend that her dad and I weren't together. I know... as I type this, I'm cringing on the inside.

We stayed the night in this really cool condo. Pixie still says it's the nicest condo she's ever seen, although if I remember correctly, it wasn't all that. Anyway, the next morning, we had to sit through the timeshare presentation before we could get the much-coveted Harry Potter tickets. We were just one hour away from the tickets. I could already taste the Butterbeer!

The manager came over, held up his phone to show me my Facebook page, and asked, "Is this your husband?" I was shocked. The guy on the highway had said it would be fine, with no issues. I felt embarrassed, as though I was in the principal's office. I said yes, and he escorted us out of the room. Pixie couldn't even finish her breakfast. They gave us valet service when we arrived, but they handed us the keys and pointed at the car upon leaving. Unfortunately, there were no Harry Potter tickets for us.

Takeaways

- Don't trust the timeshare people.
- Don't try to rope your kid into lying to someone else to get what you want. It's just embarrassing.

LET'S TAKE ACTION: Write down a time you did something that you regretted. What lesson did you learn?

____

____

____

____

SPAGHETTI STREETS

I wasn't always a risk-taker. In fact, I used to be terrified of driving on what I call "spaghetti streets"—those highways with so many lanes and exits that they resemble spaghetti crossing over each other. For many years, I avoided such highways. Then, one day, I had to drive from Dallas to Houston. I don't recall the reason, but I had Pixie with me, who was just a baby at the time, and I was terrified. I had these little puffs for toddlers, as I wanted to stay completely focused while driving. Pixie was in her car seat in the back, and I remember gripping the steering wheel as if my life depended on it. Every few minutes, I handed puffs to Pixie while navigating through traffic. After about 30 minutes, which felt like a near-death experience, I began to cheer as I finally reached the outskirts of Houston. We had made it through the spaghetti highways in one piece! As I cheered, Pixie started clapping in the back. We celebrated together.

That trip made me feel invincible. Although I still had fears when driving through traffic, my confidence grew immensely because of that journey. With Bobby working a 9-5 job, Pixie and I would take summer trips back to Florida to teach paint parties and visit family. I planned road trips for us, staying with friends or family members while driving from Texas to South Florida and back. We did this for three consecutive summers, and it was a blast. We created so many memories from those road trips, and I'm grateful for the courage to undertake them. Even though it was sometimes scary, it was also empowering. I could make money and take my daughter on fun adventures. She helped at every paint party we taught, earning her own money.

While you're building your dream, remember to find moments to spend with your family. When I was working full time and teaching paint parties on the side, I was exhausted. A few years later, I added the online aspect of the business. There were times when I was so focused on building the business that I neglected my personal life. What's the point of building if you look up and everyone you love is gone? So, make sure to spend time with the people you love, even if that means building your dream more slowly.

Takeaways

- Always remember the reason you are doing this.
- You can build your dream slower if needed so you don't sacrifice your family.
- Never underestimate the power of overcoming a fear.

LET'S TAKE ACTION: List a time when you overcame a fear. List a time when you had an adventure.

____

____

____

____

THE DREAMER ZONE

DISCOVER WHAT YOU WANT

Have you ever noticed that everyone has different things they like? For example, my cousin loves teeth and is studying to be a dentist. My other cousin is obsessed with decorating. I'll go to the fridge to get a drink, and by the time I come back, she's moved the couch. My other cousin is into baking and can make the best pastries in the world.

Man, I have a lot of cousins.

But the point is, we all have different dreams, different things that light our fire, things we are drawn to, things that fuel our soul. What is the thing that YOU always go back to?

For me, it's always been painting. When I was 15, I asked my mom if I could paint on my wall. To my surprise, she said sure! Over the next year, I spent hours working on a giant Simba from *The Lion King* on my bedroom wall. I had no idea how to mix colors or the first thing about perspective. Simba was overtaking the jungle, and it took me three tries to get his color right. I LOVED everything about that project. It gave me hope, something exciting to work on and create.

As I look back on the years from 15 to now, I've always loved painting big! Murals at schools, pools, and even roller skating rinks. I knew that painting was something I loved. It felt like an escape, and I felt like anything was possible when I looked at a giant wall and planned out a great adventure in paint. It gave me life.

Takeaways

- There are giant dreams to be had even when you are young.
- Find something that adds excitement to your life.

LET'S TAKE ACTION: What is something that gives you energy?

____

____

____

____

NASHVILLE AND ITS CHAOTIC, BEAUTIFUL NOISE

"I thought it would be more organized," Pixie, my daughter, said as we walked down Broadway in Nashville.

Every bar has a star singing their heart out, hoping to be discovered or trying to make ends meet until they make it. Nashville never disappoints, but seeing it through Pixie's eyes was really cool. We saw an artist named Andrew Gullahor who talked about finding what you love and how God will meet you there. He emphasized paying attention to the way God made you. His words were powerful because often, we think we have to be a certain way, conforming to an idea of what a "good" Christian looks like. However, in fact, God made us all different for a reason. We should lean into those differences and why you are the way you are.

A surgeon should probably be a little arrogant.

An engineer should probably be exact.

An architect should probably be detailed.

A lawyer should probably be a rule follower.

A musician should probably be a night owl.

An artist should probably be messy.

So, if you have a certain gift, stop going against it. Try leaning into your gift, and God will meet you there. What gift do you naturally have that you can lean into? Let's discover what you like. One of the easiest ways is to discover what you don't like. This is usually a faster way to get to what you really like.

For example, I HATE cold weather. Not just dislikc, but HATE.

Bobby and Pixie LOVE to snow ski and snowboard. Really, it's torture for me. Maybe it's because I didn't grow up going snow skiing, so this world was really new to me, or maybe it's because I'm not that athletic in the cold, or maybe it's just stupid. When I see people walking with their boots and skis poofed out like an over-exploded puffer fish, they never seem to be smiling. They always look miserable. As I write this book, Pixie and Bobby are snowboarding while I am in the room by the fake fire. At least it's warm, and there's a small coffee maker in my room, so I'm happy.

Whether you're on their side or mine, realizing what I dislike has been a big win in my life. I know for sure that I hate cold weather. Hallmark movies with scenes of snowball fights are really not for me. Put me in the crystal-clear waters of the Gulf of Mexico on a beautiful day in early June, and I am in my happy place. But I didn't always know that; I had to figure it out.

Here's what I've learned that hopefully will help you: Most people won't take the time to really examine what they don't like. They go through life repeating the same activities because they don't acknowledge that these things make them miserable. When I discovered how to identify the things I don't like, it opened up the things I like!

Below, you can use the space provided to write about things you don't like. DO NOT focus on what you *do* like right now, only on what you don't like.

I'll go first:

Things I DON'T like:

Cold Weather.

Skateboarding.

Seafood.

Running. Man, I hate running.

Going to a gym.

Rude people.

Takeaways

- Cold weather sucks.
- Finding out what you dislike is powerful.

LET'S TAKE ACTION: Your turn. Things you DON'T like:

____

____

____

____

VOLLEYBALL PRO

Now that we know what we DON'T like, let's discover what we DO like. This is part of the ADVENTURE of the Dreamer!

You can approach this exercise in many ways, but curiosity is the best approach. Also, remember that you don't have to be good at something to enjoy it.

Writing this in my mid-40s, I've realized that I LOVE the ocean. Not just like, but LOVE. I'm a self-proclaimed mermaid, and if there's clear water within 100 feet of me, I am in it! It fuels my soul. I've also realized I like warm weather with clear water. Some people hate sand, salty air, and heat. Not this girl. Give me a 90-degree day with full sun, beautiful clear water, and a cold drink, and I'm in heaven!

I also like to joke that in another life, I would be a professional beach volleyball player. Being a benchwarmer on the B team in high school, I was rarely called in to play. However, years later, as an art teacher, we had a teacher volleyball game in front of the students. I still remember playing that game and actually being okay. I wasn't good, but I felt awesome! I came home that day and told my husband I was the star of the team! Although this may not be entirely true, in a sense, I felt like a superhero. I wasn't sitting on the bench, AND I could return the ball. I even spiked it once. It was pretty cool. So now, with my daughter, I often volley, and again, that feeling of doing something I love strikes me.

What's really cool about life that we often forget is that we get to figure out who we are and what makes us tick. It's part of the adventure and the curiosity of life. What's something that makes you excited? Were you really good at roller skating back in the day? (By the way, I'm really good! LOL)

Have you tried pickleball, not just in a professional way, but by making it fun with silly headbands and pretending to take it really seriously?

I heard this saying years ago, and it still rings true today: "You can either be an inspiration to people or a warning of what not to be or do." I hope I can be the inspiration, not the warning. Which are you? And which do you want to be?

Takeaways

- Buy fluorescent pickleball headbands.
- If you can be anything in life, be a mermaid.
- Curiosity is the best approach.

LET'S TAKE ACTION: Name three things you DO like. For example: Warm weather, swimming in the ocean, roller skating, etc.

____

____

____

____

WHO CAN I TELL ABOUT THIS DREAM/ADVENTURE?

This, my friend, is one of life's mysteries.

I've learned the hard way about who to share my crazy, wild dreams with. It's a hard lesson you will learn, too, but hopefully, this will help take the sting away. Many people will be your biggest supporters when you are failing, but as success comes, jealousy may creep up.

I've also learned that not everyone needs to know what your dreams and goals are. Some people will immediately change the subject. Others will say, "That's cool," and then talk about what they did yesterday. Then there's the rare friend, or if you're lucky enough to have a few of these friends, they will support you and jump in with you! I am pretty lucky to have a few of these friends.

One of my oldest friends, Alyson, of nearly two decades, has been a part of all my crazy since the beginning. She has helped with surfboards, that essential oil phase I was in, a year of setting up booths around town squares, and with all of our Painted Proms. When I excitedly say, "Let's rent a horse and maybe some baby goats!" she starts looking up vendors. When I had a vision for a circus-themed Painted Prom, she found the tent and cotton candy! I mean, this girl is on a mission. She's organized, smart, and always has my back.

Another friend of mine is my "ride-or-die!" Even if she doesn't agree with my crazy idea, she allows me to talk all about it! It may calm down after I sleep on it, but in the moment, she lets me have it. I think that's such a great quality. Gretchen always takes time to listen to my "crazy." If it doesn't work out, she will say, "You don't know until you try," always using life as one big test. I love it!

I've had other friends I share something fun with, and it's met with fear, negativity, overwhelm, or they just change the subject. I used to let that bother me, but now I just make a mental note, and I'm more cautious of who I let into that part of my life. I think that's one of the biggest lessons for taking action through fear that I've learned: you have to fight for your vision! It's not their dream; it's yours! Why should they be as excited as you are? **Don't put the responsibility on someone else to carry the excitement of your dream!**

Takeaways

- Nothing can replace a great friend.
- Always fight for your dreams.

LET'S TAKE ACTION: Remember to react kindly to others as they share their dreams. Treat others how you want to be treated. Often referred to as the "Golden Rule," it is a fundamental moral guideline that suggests we should interact with others in a manner we would like others to interact with us.

Who is your go-to friend?

____

____

____

____

CHOOSE YOUR WORDS WISELY

Many people have said, "Life is only as good as your mindset," but what exactly does that mean? I've read hundreds of books on mindset, business, human behavior, happiness, being organized, self-help, the law of attraction, and so on. But what does it really mean to have a great mindset?

Well, you're in luck! I'm going to break it down into *3 Success Tips* to help you create a great mindset, which in turn will help you create a great life. Learning about this has significantly changed my life, and I hope it will help you, too. My daily routine involves creating habits that control my thoughts to help my outcomes. Now, you may think I'm getting all weird on you, but I'm just talking about small daily habits that can significantly change your daily experiences! Are you ready?

Habit: *an acquired mode of behavior that has become nearly or completely involuntary. (Merriam-Webster)*

This is a simple way to add intentional habits that will help you ultimately change your life but not feel like a burden. For example, when I'm on a long drive or even folding clothes, I listen to my favorite podcasts. When I'm going for a walk in the morning with my dog, I listen to a new business strategy or my favorite YouTube person. You see, I'm still doing the NORMAL things I would do, but I'm adding in positive things to help my mind.

We need to ALWAYS be learning! Always!

The Internet has really made it easy to learn and connect with tons of like-minded people. Whether it's cooking, art, fitness, business, finance, or even teaching paint parties like myself, there are resources out there for you.

And the beauty of it is that YOU GET TO CHOOSE what you allow in your mind! Choose the positive ones! Get excited about something! Anything positive that brings you joy!

"Happiness is not a goal. It's a by-product of a life well lived"
- Eleanor Roosevelt

3 Success Tips

TIP #1: Influence - What are you allowing to influence your mind?

We all have 24 hours in a day and unlimited access to tons of trash. Large parts of our world feel broken, and now, more than ever, we need to protect our little "bubble."

I'm not saying I have this perfectly figured out. Hey, I love the TV show *Love is Blind* just as much as the next person, but you have to be careful about what you put in your mind. Netflix is a great example; it's a cheap way to get a ton of shows, but some of them go way too far. I don't need or want to see some of that stuff. Just because a show is highly recommended doesn't mean it's always good for your mind.

Here's what I suggest: Take notice of HOW YOU FEEL after watching a show. Are you inspired, happy, excited, OR are you depressed, disturbed, or maybe even a little ashamed? I've watched shows before that I knew were bad for me. It's easy to ignore and just say, "Everyone is doing it," but the truth is, *average* people are doing it. Do you want to be average? OR do you want a different life? A happy life? I pray for God's favor on my family, and I know when I finish a show that makes me feel depressed or ashamed, I try to reevaluate if it's necessary in my life.

Another example: There is a show called *Hoarders,* and every time I watch it, I feel sad. It makes my entire room and my house feel dark, and I feel lonely. I usually turn it off within minutes because I don't want to feel that way. It's usually accompanied by a whirlwind of 30 minutes of donation cleaning up around the house, removing extra mugs, shoes, clothes, etc.!

So… TRY THIS!

Instead of going with the flow and just watching whatever is popular, CHOOSE! Yes, we still have that option. Select shows that will leave you excited and inspired. There are a ton out there! Some of my favorites are *Shark Tank* and *The Amazing Race.*

Other things that have totally transformed my life are reading, podcasts, and YouTube. Some of my favorite books are *Jesus Calling* by Sarah Young for a quick morning Bible study, *Big Magic: Creative Living Beyond Fear* by Elizabeth Gilbert, and *The War of Art* by Steven Pressfield. I'm also obsessed with podcasts: *Dave Ramsey* to help me get back on track with my finances and *Ed Mylett* for personal development. My favorite YouTube go-tos when I need a much-needed attitude adjustment are Joyce Meyer and Tony Robbins. I'm constantly finding new books and podcasts to fuel my mind.

"You're always one decision away from a totally different life."
- Unknown

TIP #2: WHO are YOU allowing to Influence YOU?

Family, friends, well-meaning co-workers? Now, hear me out. Family is family, and we all want to keep the peace. Also, friends are so valuable too. I've heard several times that we are the combination of the five closest people we surround ourselves with. Who are you normally around?

Have you ever been around someone who can give you ten reasons why they can't do something, usually in one breath?

Well, I don't know about you, but it's exhausting to listen to. When I would have a bad attitude, my sweet hubby would joke, "You would complain if you won the lottery, and they told you it was the cash option!" He said that about five times before it hit me that I was complaining about stupid stuff. It was a habit that I didn't even know I had developed, and it was exhausting him in the process.

Whatever consumes your mind controls your life. Read that again out loud so you can really take it in. *Whatever consumes your mind controls your life.*

TIP #3: Find Your People

Focus on your fellow dreamer. They are out there. Sometimes, it feels like you are all alone. Find that collection of people who will dream with you. There are people who dream like you. Go out and find them. Remember, deviating from the norm WILL make you stand out! Sometimes, it can isolate you. Also, when people see others making positive changes, they may feel it reflects negatively on them, like a mirror effect. Your making different changes might make them feel guilty about not making changes themselves. You can't control other people; you can only control your reactions to them.

"When do I start this change to a greater mindset?" you ask. Every day is a new opportunity to start changing your mindset. "But Heidi, it's overwhelming, and I don't know where to start!"

Always, and forever, start with gratitude. I know—it's dorky and overused, but it's powerful. This is always the first and easiest place to start: in every situation, in every moment, in every new day. Always!

One day, our water was turned off. For about three hours, I tried to wash my hands, no water. Start the dishwasher; no water. *I'm going to take a quick shower—oh CRAP, still NO WATER!* Then, as my daughter complained, I reminded her, "Just think how blessed we are. Lots of people in the world have to walk miles and miles to get water daily. We just have a small inconvenience." It totally made us appreciate it more.

It may be hard at first to be thankful each day. You may have experienced the worst of the worst. I pray for peace for you in whatever you are going through. I believe God has a plan for all of us—not to perish, but to prosper. So, whatever the challenge, the situation, the grief, the pain, you still have a God that loves you and an opportunity to always help someone else, maybe going through something similar.

A sweet friend of mine was in a tragic car accident that caused a fatality. In her trauma and total guilt and sadness for the family who lost a loved one, she slowly started taking steps to reach out and help others in a similar situation. It's an extremely emotional time for all involved, and she is using gratitude and serving others to help heal. She has now written a book called *Left Turn, Life Unimagined,* and she hosts a podcast designed to help others who are CADI (Causing Accidental Death or Injury).

In an unimaginable tragedy, she is daily taking steps to help others find their purpose again.

Takeaways

- Notice how you feel when things influence your mind.
- Choose what you allow to influence your mind.
- Always be learning.
- Find your people.

LET'S TAKE ACTION: *What* are you letting influence your mind? *Who* are you letting influence your mind? Write down the good and the bad influences. *Who* are the people in your life who are your biggest support system? If you don't have those people in your life, where could you go, in person or online, to find someone who dreams like you?

____

____

____

____

READERS ARE LEADERS!

Instill the habit of reading every day in your life and your kids' lives! You'll be amazed at the mindset changes you can achieve by reading the right books. I didn't start reading until my early 30s. Initially, I laughed off my husband's suggestion of reading every night because I was accustomed to falling asleep with the TV on. However, over the past several years, I've read hundreds of books, and the amount of knowledge and information available is astounding. Initially, it was just sappy romances by Nicholas Sparks. But as my business grew, I yearned for a change in my mindset. I began devouring as many books as I could, and I noticed not just my business transforming but also my general life attitude.

You might already be a habitual reader—after all, you've made it this far in the book—but make sure you're reading materials that enhance your life. Just like TV, books can introduce negative elements. I make it a point to mix in some fiction occasionally, or else I'd be perpetually stuck on business and mindset books. Remember to take a break and enjoy some well-written stories as well.

"Socrates demonstrated long ago that the truly free individual is free only to the extent of his own self-mastery. While those who will not govern themselves are condemned to find masters to govern over them."
— Steven Pressfield, The War of Art

Takeaways

- Make reading a habit.
- Seek self-discipline.

LET'S TAKE ACTION: What was the last book you read, and how did you feel after you read it?

____

____

____

____

I OWE YOU MONEY?

I've been lucky enough to have a lot of family support for my crazy dreams, although I know that's not always the case.

My husband, Bobby, always listens and lets me express the wildest ideas in my head. Even if he doesn't believe they're possible, he lets me talk through them, which has been a godsend! For a few years, my father-in-law and I had a business arrangement where I would pay him to make 16X20 inch pallet boards that I could use as a canvas for my paint parties. He would search all over town, making canvas-sized pallet boards. He had a list of places to visit after work and on weekends, collecting pallets from construction sites, businesses, etc. When I came to pick up a few for upcoming parties, one day, he said, "No, you can't have any today."

Confused, I asked, "Why? I have a paint party this week, and I need 50."

He calmly explained, "You haven't paid for the ones you already picked up."

He was right; I had taken advantage of his kindness.

Still needing 50 for my party and without money to pay him, he let me use his shop. My sweet hubby and I cut and assembled 50 pallets, with my father-in-law helping out. He's great like that—teaching lessons but always showing up to help. The paint party for 50 happened; I paid what I owed and learned a very big lesson. Now, I hate owing anyone anything.

Takeaways

- Debt = Stress.
- Don't take advantage of someone's kindness.

LET'S TAKE ACTION: Do you owe anyone money that you need to repay? You should pay it back even if they are not asking for it. You borrowed it, and it's ultimately your responsibility.

____

____

____

____

WHAT WOULD DOLLY DO?

Dolly Parton is a force of nature, generously giving millions of her fortune to causes she cares about, such as education, The Imagination Library (a book gifting program that mails free books to children), and many others. She marches to the beat of her own drum and doesn't judge others.

My respect for Dolly and the way she lives her life has always been high, but it soared on Thanksgiving Day in 2023. My mother-in-law, a die-hard Cowboys fan who adores everything about them, convinced us to buy tickets to the Cowboys' Thanksgiving football game. Although I wasn't overly excited, I thought it would be a fun shared experience, so we were in!

About three weeks later, I heard that Dolly was set to perform the halftime show at the Dallas Cowboys Stadium. Saying I was excited would be a massive understatement—"Operation Dolly" was in full swing! Many people were there to see the Cowboys play, but I had one purpose only: a Dolly Concert!

We spent several days making jerseys that said "DOLLY" with the number 95 on them. Using glitter craft paper and a hot glue gun, we added dashes between the 9 and 5 (9 5) to represent her famous movie *9 to 5*. I painted a Dolly mural on posterboard, and my daughter and mother-in-law painted *"HERE FOR DOLLY"* on the signs. We held them up like crazy people at every opportunity! Then, halftime arrived! Dolly appeared on stage, wearing the Dallas Cowboys Cheerleaders uniform! At 77 years old, she was rocking the cheerleaders' uniform. This was the moment I realized that anything is possible. She went on to perform hits like "9-5," "Jolene," and even "We Are the Champions!" My daughter and I screamed and sang along, and I'm pretty sure a few tears flowed. I felt like Dolly, whom I've admired for so many years, had just raised the bar again. It was as if any excuses you might have had went out the window. My mind buzzed with excitement about the possibilities of a life well-lived.

Now, we know that Dolly is a legend. She broke the mold, created the exact life she wanted, and is still pushing boundaries on what's acceptable, all while trying not to offend anyone. She is one of my greatest examples of sharing God's love through your talents, spreading joy and hope while living a good life. I've never met anyone who spoke ill of Dolly. The main lesson I've learned from her is to chase what you want. She always talks about dreaming big and working hard to make things happen. *That* is the difference.

Also, here's something to consider for self-awareness: When you see someone else succeed, do you feel jealous or excited? For example, I've noticed people in my life who feel jealous when they see someone else succeed. This mindset is a dangerous place to live. Instead, I recommend the following approach: When I see someone succeed, especially in something I love, my initial reaction is, *If they can do it, so can I.* It's similar to what happened with Roger Bannister, the man who ran the first sub-four-minute mile. Once he achieved it, many others followed and did the same. His achievement *proved* it could be done! Nobody had done it before him, so the belief was that it was impossible. Once proven possible, it became achievable for anyone.

To be honest, sometimes I think you can dream too big. But then I'm reminded that Dolly spent a lifetime creating her dream life. If you reflect on your life 5, 10, or 20 years ago, is it the same? No, you are changing, growing, discovering, learning, seeking, and doing so much more. Are you becoming the person you aspire to be, or are you letting life make decisions for you? Let's take inspiration from Dolly: dream big, take massive action, and create the life you want. I want to look back on my life and smile, knowing that I chose how to react to my situations and to create the life that God intended for me.

Takeaways

- Dolly is a legend.
- Age is just a number.

LET'S TAKE ACTION: Who is your Dolly? Who do you look up to? What traits about that person do you admire? How can you become more like them?

DO IT ANYWAY

Most people will never see your "behind the scenes"—the countless hours of dreaming, planning, creating, growing, and failing. And that's okay. Do it anyway. One of my favorite poems is "Do it Anyway" by Mother Teresa. My daughter Pixie had to memorize this for a speech meet in 7th grade. It left a lasting impression on me. I hope it inspires you to keep chasing your dream, whatever it may be. This is the Version found written on the wall in Mother Teresa's home for children in Calcutta:

People are often unreasonable, irrational, and self-centered.

Forgive them anyway.

If you are kind, people may accuse you of selfish, ulterior motives.

Be kind anyway.

If you are successful, you will win some unfaithful friends and some genuine enemies. *Succeed anyway.*

If you are honest and sincere, people may deceive you.

Be honest and sincere anyway.

What you spend years creating, others could destroy overnight.

Create Anyway.

If you find serenity and happiness, some may be jealous.

Be happy anyway.

The good you do today, will often be forgotten.

Do good anyway.

Give the best you have, and it will never be enough.

Give your best anyway.

In the final analysis, it is between you and God.

It was never between you and them anyway.

- St. Teresa of Calcutta (Mother Teresa), "Do It Anyway"

Takeaways

- Don't let other people's opinions stop your progress.
- Always be the best at whatever you are called to do.

LET'S TAKE ACTION: What is something in your life that you stopped doing because you were afraid of other people's opinions?

____

____

____

____

"MONEY ISN'T EVERYTHING" TELL THAT TO SOMEONE WHO IS BROKE

My mom used to joke, "Money isn't everything unless you don't have any." I feel this to my core. Coming from a big family, I am the middle child among three brothers and one sister. My mom had my oldest brother when she was just 14 years old, followed by another brother a few years later. After divorcing a really bad man, she met my wonderful dad. With two daughters and another son, their family was complete. Five kids sharing one bathroom in a small house meant pretty much constant chaos. We shared rooms, slept wherever, and I didn't even know there was a top and bottom sheet until I got married. Most of the time, we just grabbed a blanket and slept on the floor or wherever we landed. It was a fun life! I mean, who needs a fancy top sheet anyway?

My mom always struggled with mental illness, and looking back on her life after she passed, I have so much more grace for her now. She wasn't a 14-year-old wanting to start a family; that was forced on her. Seeing her life in a different light makes me wish I had the grace for her then, which I do now. But my older two brothers were meant to be here. I love them so much, all of my siblings. Sometimes, I wish I had given Pixie a sibling, but that wasn't how it happened, and there's no use wasting energy on regrets. Instead, I take her around my family a lot so she can enjoy the awesome chaos that a big family brings.

My husband once asked me, "How did you know to dream for a different life?" For example, my favorite restaurant was Long John Silver's. I had never heard of, let alone been to, a Chili's until I started dating Bobby. He's an only child and had access to a completely different life than I did. It doesn't mean his way was better or our way was worse; they were just different.

My family is loud and inappropriate. We laugh when we shouldn't, and we talk when we shouldn't. The first time I went to Bobby's family's place, it was so quiet—weirdly, politely quiet. I didn't understand that world. We weren't showing love if we weren't making fun of each other. As I've gotten older, I've realized the pros and cons of a big and smaller family.

For me, those words my mom said so many years ago stuck with me: "Money isn't everything unless you don't have any." Being in a big family with my dad working and my mom staying home, money was tight. We all had jobs early on, and a strong work ethic was instilled from the time I was a little girl. We were taught the normal way: work, borrow, pay back; work, borrow, pay back. It was a grind. I didn't know any other way. Buried in student loan debt, car payments, maxed-out credit cards, living paycheck to paycheck, bankruptcy, and several other moves led us to the Cherry Street house. This small, 800-square-foot rental house was where I finally started getting mad, realizing that if I wanted a certain life, no one was going to hand it to me—I had to earn it. I wanted Pixie not to have student loans for college. I wanted to be able to travel, pick my own schedule, and not worry when I was at the grocery store.

Recently, Pixie was helping me clean out my closet, and we came across a note that said:

"When this happens, I will feel successful:
Groceries in the fridge
Massage every month
Debt Free
Tide Detergent and Tostitos Chips
Someone to help clean the house
Traveling every year"

When I look at this note, it doesn't mention a private jet, fancy bags, or designer shoes. It lists the things I wanted to feel successful. Each of us has a different idea of success. I truly believe we go through levels in life. I always picture the video game Mario Brothers and the moments when I would get a "Power Up." That's how life feels to me: We go through life, and sometimes we get a promotion (Power Up), sometimes a perfect day (Power Up), and sometimes things just fall into place (Power Up). As we learn lessons, it's as if we advance to another level.

Takeaways

- Money doesn't buy you happiness.
- Success looks different for everyone.
- If you are not currently at the success you want, it's time to "Power Up."

LET'S TAKE ACTION: What is on your list that makes YOU feel successful? What is a way to take action and "Power Up."

____

____

____

____

THAT TIME I TRIED TO SELL A FAMOUS PERSON ESSENTIAL OILS

Yep, I tried. Here's the thing I appreciate about myself: I take action fast. The thing I don't appreciate is that sometimes, it makes me look foolish. However, I've learned that I can grow and learn even through those foolish times.

I had a professional relationship with someone I admire very much. She met me for lunch one day and gave me business advice. I've always looked up to her. As an artist and creative person, I sometimes have "squirrel moments," you know, trying to focus on ten things at once but getting nothing done. Well, my business was going okay, and I ended up getting "squirreled" into selling essential oils. I love them and use them daily, but selling them wasn't what I LOVED to do. It wasn't my passion, like painting. However, for the next 18 months, I was on a mission to sell oils.

Looking back, it makes me cringe, but I know we've all been there. Maybe not with oils, but with makeup, vitamins, CBD, hair products, weight loss, nails—the list goes on. I've been involved with many of them. However, this time, I took it too far. I contacted this famous person and asked if I could sell oils at her event. She was very polite and responded, "Heidi, I love your entrepreneurial spirit, but I don't think it's the right fit." She was so sweet and let me down with a quick no. It was one of the first times I realized I could just tell people no.

Being a recovering people pleaser, I always felt I needed an ironclad reason why I couldn't do something, why I couldn't be involved in everything OTHER people were asking of me. When I heard her so easily reply with no, it hurt for a second, and then MAD respect hit me! I truly appreciated how easily she was able to say that and move on.

So, the next time you are faced with an opportunity to say yes but you REALLY want to say no, it's okay. Say no if it doesn't align with what you are trying to do.

Takeaways

- Don't be a people pleaser.
- Be careful of "squirrel moments" and not losing focus.
- "No" is a complete sentence.

LET'S TAKE ACTION: What can you say no to this month that doesn't align with the life you want to create?

____

____

____

____

NO ONE IS COMING TO SAVE YOU

This may be hard to hear, but I want you to know. For many years in my life, I thought a person, a thing, or an opportunity would be what would get me out of my financial situation. I had this feeling that someone else would make my dream happen. If I could just meet the right people, get into the right circle, be interviewed by a certain podcast, this would take me where I needed to be. But the harsh truth is, I've had many of those things happen, and while they're helpful, they're not what will create the life you want. No one is coming to save you. YOU have to create the life you want.

Married two weeks after I turned 18 years old, I was a child bride in today's terms. Madly in love with Bobby, but we were just babies! He was 20, and I was 18 when we married.

Not really having the tools to create our definition of a successful life, we lived paycheck to paycheck, usually borrowing $50 here and there from parents to make it to the next week. We always paid them back but were always struggling. Even when we made decent money, we would have moments at the mall, picking out a pair of sunglasses and literally asking ourselves, *Groceries this week or sunglasses?* (Obviously, we would pick the sunglasses.) Most of the time, we ate garlic bread for dinner. It was our specialty. We used generic hamburger buns, buttered them, topped them with garlic salt and cheese, and put them in the oven under the broiler. Within five minutes, dinner was ready!

One night, we forgot to set the timer, and one minute too long meant dinner was burnt to a crisp. Hungry, we picked off the burnt top and ate the bread. But back then, I remember caring less about food and more about getting that new pair of sunglasses.

Then, life kept coming. Things happened.

Several years later in our life, after moving back to Texas, it really hit me.

I needed to go to Florida to see a family member and couldn't afford the plane ticket. I missed out on being there for my family because I couldn't figure out how to get my finances in order. This was after the bankruptcy, and we were still struggling to make ends meet. My husband and I are both spenders, so it takes a lot of discipline. I learned that your finances and habits don't change overnight, kind of like with pregnancy and weight loss. It takes nine months to gain weight when pregnant; it takes time to lose it too. This was very true with our finances. We got into that situation because we struggled, and now I had a huge setback and couldn't be there for my family.

This realization hit me like a ton of bricks. I started researching how people become millionaires. I know it sounds cheesy, but I wasn't raised in a place where people had money. I was taught an extreme work ethic. Since I was 15, I've always had a job and responsibilities. I knew how to go to work and how to bring home a paycheck, but I knew nothing about making significant money. However, I did know how to spend it fast. This search led me to many discoveries. I found out that most millionaires have seven streams of income. At the time, I was teaching part-time and running paint parties full-time. My husband had a full-time job, but to say we had anywhere near multiple streams of income would be an understatement.

One of the things I am thankful for is the Internet. I know it has some crazy stuff on it, but it also offers a lot of great information if you seek it. I was on a mission, spending every extra moment I had searching for ways to generate additional streams of revenue. This search led me to an online event that taught me how to make money online. Before I knew it, I was signed up for a year-long program learning how to build an email list. In my head, I had an amount I wanted to make. At the time, we lived in an 800-square-foot rental house. I had written *"$30,000 a month"* on a posterboard and taped it to my door. My husband saw it and never made fun of me for it. He didn't know exactly how I would do it, but he had faith that I could. I think it's so important that sometimes you need someone else to believe in you more than you do.

Why did I think I could do it? I mean, $30,000 a month is a crazy high number. This was one of those moments where I remember hearing someone online saying, *"Once you make $30,000 a month, that's plenty of money to do whatever you want."* So, nowhere near that number at the time, I wrote it as a goal. It took many years to reach that goal, but it happened. Now, I have a new number written by my door that I look at every day in my office.

Takeaways

- Sometimes you need someone to believe in you more than you believe in yourself.
- It's okay to dream REALLY big.

LET'S TAKE ACTION: Have you had a time in your life when you felt like you had to take things into your own hands?

____

____

____

____

ANXIETY IS MY SUPERPOWER

Do you struggle with anxiety? I have since my mid-20s. It seems to get worse at night and sometimes turns into panic attacks. During the pandemic, I was in a store with Bobby on one side of me and Pixie on the other, and I was in a corner. Wearing a mask heightened my anxiety, and I felt I couldn't breathe. In a panic, I tried to get out of the area to have space. Although it only took a second for them to move, it felt as if time had changed to slow motion; every sound got louder, and the room got smaller. I finally escaped to the outside of the store, ripped off my mask, and started breathing in and out to try and calm myself. Most of the time, my anxiety is a restless feeling of always wanting to do more and be more, which, in many ways, is a blessing. However, that energy has also left me feeling exhausted and overwhelmed.

Garth Brooks once said there is a blessing and a curse to everything. You may have the blessing of doing more and being more, but you'll also have the curse of doing more and being more and the responsibilities that attach to that identity. Another wise man, Dave Ramsey, said in a podcast that it's hard for the warrior to rest after the war is over, referring to the struggle to survive financially. I like to think of his words and also add the struggle to fit in, to feel worthy, and the struggle to be a good wife, mother, daughter, friend, Christian, artist, business owner, etc. It's overwhelming and guilt-ridden. It can be the thing that drives you or the thing that tears you down.

So many times in my life, I've made choices based on what I thought someone else would want me to do, choices that were easy and comfortable. I've realized that as I make bigger choices, the anxiety is still present. It can keep me second-guessing every life choice I've made, leading me down a rabbit hole that helps no one and also makes me feel a little insane.

In the same breath, I treasure the anxiety because I know it fills my soul with energy and an overwhelming feeling of urgency that I am made for so many great things by our Creator. It's almost as if the quicker I can get through lessons, the faster I can move on to another set of challenges, goals, and bigger realized dreams.

But what is life if only an endless to-do list? What is life if you don't take time to rest and be still from time to time, to listen to God's lead, to take it all in, to actually stop and celebrate how far you've come, and to be grateful for the one who gave it all to you in the first place? My new prayer over the past few months has been for God to fill me with overwhelming inspiration, to help me rest, and to find ways to handle my anxiety. Maybe not get rid of it entirely, as I think it has a big purpose in my life, but to continue to inspire me with a sense of urgency to do great things. And to learn to sit and just create.

As I have watched the world change over the past several months in every way, it's given me a new perspective. We are all just here, passing through for a very short time. What would you do if you were told you only had THIS year? Where would you go? What are those big, scary, anxiety-filled dreams you think will never happen? What if those big, scary dreams COULD happen? Would it be worth trying? I think so. I think God wants us to continue growing and pushing ourselves, even when it may make us uncomfortable or give us anxiety.

Takeaways

- You can find a blessing and a curse in everything.
- Pray when you're overwhelmed.
- Life is short, so live it to your potential.

LET'S TAKE ACTION: What's a trait in which you have always seen the negative? For me, it was always anxiety. How can you change your viewpoint to make it a positive?

____

____

____

____

UNCERTAINTY

Are you feeling uncertain right now? As much as the world can grip you with a feeling of uncertainty, remember that His mercies are new every morning.

God never changes, and He knows how it all ends. Instead of sitting in our uncertainty and fear, which can cause anxiety and other unwanted emotions, give them to God. Let Him help you along.

I know it's easier said than done, but you always have to remember: It's easy to have faith when everything is going right, but it's hard when it seems like everything is uncertain.

As my daughter nears graduation, I am uncertain about where she will end up. Having spent 18 years raising her, she's now ready to fly. The uncertainty of where she will land can cause me anxiety and fear about the future.

Here are a couple of things I'm doing that may help you if you're feeling uncertain.

1. **Write letters to God:** Your fears, your anxieties, your gratitude. Tell Him everything!
2. **Remember that God is in control:** Not you. When we let go of our need to control everything and put it in His hands, we can start to see a path again.

1 Peter 5:7 says, *"Cast all your anxiety on him because he cares for you."*

Takeaways

- There will be times in life when we are uncertain, but we still trust God's plan.
- We are never totally in control.

LET'S TAKE ACTION: What can you do today to help your feeling of uncertainty?

____

____

____

____

YOU WILL FALL ON YOUR FACE

Have you ever done something scary, hoping you wouldn't fall flat on your face? Well, I did something big in my business, and to be honest, I was a little (maybe a lot) terrified to launch it! But, as God always shows me, on the other side of fear is something magical. Every year, I host a giant event for all the people inside Paint Party Headquarters. We meet in person to learn and paint together! This particular event was one of the biggest things I've ever done. I rented out the Dolly Suite at DreamMore Resorts in the Smoky Mountains and hosted a giant event. I also added "Live from the Dolly Suite," which was very well received. It helped ladies who really wanted to come to Paint Party Business Live at Dollywood in person have a small piece of the experience without the travel. It was all terrifying, but I knew I had to take action through fear to make big dreams and goals happen. I know God wants good things for us. I used to feel I wasn't deserving of good things. How many of you have thought that sometimes? It makes me sad to think that I thought that way for so long. I hope you are not in that position.

God really does want good things for us, not just good, but GREAT! A lady once told me to pray for forgiveness for all the anxiety I was carrying around. Then, thank God for all that He is giving me. That hit me like a ton of bricks. I thought, *Dang, I was totally not being a good receiver of the many gifts He was giving me because I didn't feel deserving of them.* So now, even if I'm scared, I will still take action and be thankful for the opportunity to try something cool, even if it fails!

Several times in my life I took action through fear and God over-delivered.

"Every good and perfect gift is from above, coming down from the Father of the heavenly lights, who does not change like shifting shadows." James 1:17

Ask God for help, seek His guidance, and take massive action. BUT don't forget to BE THANKFUL before, during, and after He gives you all of these gifts!

Takeaways

- Don't hold unnecessary anxiety about things that you know God doesn't want you to hold.
- Take action through fear.

LET'S TAKE ACTION: Have you ever felt undeserving of a gift you've been given? How can you change the feeling to gratitude instead of undeserving?

____

____

____

____

CHASING YOUR DREAMS CAN BE LONELY

Feeling left out sucks! Meeting new people can be hard, but I know the awkwardness is worth the headache, especially when you meet the right people. Don't let fear stop you.

I remember trying to make a new friend at Michaels. Yep, the arts and crafts store. I thought it was perfect! She's into art, I'm into art. Score! When you're older, why does it feel so hard to meet new people? I think it's the rejection feeling. We don't like it, therefore we don't put ourselves out there. Anyway, My husband and daughter were with me, rooting me on. They went down another aisle so I could "try and make a friend." My palms were sweaty, and I went to ask if she wanted to paint together sometime. She said yes!!!! We exchanged numbers, and I was beaming with excitement for this newfound friendship.

Nope! Rejected!

I texted a few times, and she ghosted me. Then I saw her at Michaels, and it was awkward. She said she was sorry but was really busy. In my head, I'm thinking, *We're all busy, but it takes two to make a friendship work.*

So, I didn't paint with her. We never created a friendship. I could have given up, but I didn't. The most worthwhile pursuits, the greatest joys in life, are often harder to reach. When you see a great friendship, it's an example of work: hours, months, or even years of endless conversation, lots of laughter, and being there for one another. One of the things we crave most on this earth, being accepted by others, can get shortchanged when we're in the thick of it, raising kids, working nonstop, building a business, being a mom, wife, sister, daughter, whatever. We let friendships slide.

Years later, our kids move out, life looks different, and we wonder why we didn't devote more time to friendships. But the good news is, it's NEVER too late to find a friend and be a friend. No matter how old you are, there are other people seeking and praying for a friend.

My challenge to you is to seek and pray for a friend. If one doesn't work out (like my Michaels girl), keep trying. There's the right friend out there for you. Just think of ALL the adventures to come! All the excitement you have to look forward to. There will be times when it still feels weird, awkward, even lonely, but I always think that's the enemy trying to rob our joy. Don't let it. The Bible talks about friendships multiple times, so I believe God thinks it's important, too.

So here's to you: taking risks, making moves, and daring greatly. Get to know some people, step outside your comfort zone, and most importantly, find a great person to be a great friend to. You never know where a great friendship will take you.

Takeaways

- It's never too late to find a friend and be a friend.
- Pray for a friend.
- When it feels awkward, you're on the right track.

LET'S TAKE ACTION: What friend have you been neglecting? Reach out to them with a quick text to tell them hi and ask how they are doing. Maybe even invite them out for coffee.

____

____

____

____

ORGANIZED CHAOS

Organizing is hard, especially for a dreamer and an artist, so building a business can feel almost impossible. The dreamer/artist in me has the organizational skills of a raccoon. I have 100 journals scattered all over the house, Post-it notes by my bed (in case an idea strikes in the middle of the night), and endless papers and notes piled everywhere. My brain goes in all different directions at any moment. My husband bought me an Apple Watch one day, and it lasted for about 12 minutes. The notifications almost caused a mental breakdown, and then it told me when to breathe. (As I write this, I realize I am holding my breath. Maybe I do need it after all.)

Anyway, the point is, in order to be successful in business as a creative, I had to figure out a way to create in the chaos. I realized my mind likes to work in 100 journals, with paper calendars and plenty of Post-its for the middle of the night. Instead of working AGAINST my natural tendencies, I learned how to work with them. I accept that I need to write things down. I accept that there will be notes everywhere. And that's okay. I used to think that I ALWAYS had to go back through the notes, but I've learned as I've grown my company that it's okay not to go back through them. They are there if I need them, but my brain has a little break knowing I got the idea out and it's not lost.

Takeaways

- Create in the chaos.
- Work with your natural tendencies.
- We are all created differently for a reason.

LET'S TAKE ACTION: What is a trait you have that drives you nuts!? Is it something you can change? If not, how can you make peace and work with it, not against it?

___

___

___

___

100-YEAR-OLD HIPS

We are all a one-woman (or one-man) show when we start our business. In the beginning, we usually don't have a lot of help. We can almost create a sense of pride and ownership by doing everything ourselves—until we burn out.

This happened to me a few times, but one of the most significant moments was when I was teaching full-time and running my paint party business on nights and weekends. Having 850 art students a week was fun but also exhausting. I'm a self-proclaimed empath and feel everything, as most artists do. We can be sensitive souls.

One Sunday afternoon, I was lying on the couch face-first, telling Bobby I didn't think I could do this. I had no idea how I was going to go to work tomorrow. I had run myself ragged. The whole weekend was spent creating paintings for a much-needed paint party, unpacking from a previous paint party, grocery shopping, and trying to be an okay mom and okay wife.

As I lay there, my hips were in pain, and I felt like I was 100 years old. My body was shutting down, telling me to slow down. What I realized during this time was that I had to get better at scheduling my time. If I'm with Pixie and Bobby, I'm 100% with them. If I'm working, I'm 100% working. I still struggle with this today, but I try to schedule at least 4-6 days off a month (usually weekends or a Friday) to take time to regroup, rest, recharge, spend time with family, etc. I also learned that the way one person rests isn't the same as another.

For example, Bobby LOVES a day watching TV. Give that guy a great YouTube series about working on cars, and he is hooked! Me? If I'm in bed watching TV, I must be sick. There must be something wrong. So, my rest day looks more like this: I grab a coffee and walk around Barnes & Noble. I love a good bookstore or a walk through Marshalls or Home Goods. A new coffee mug or picture frame makes my heart happy. I'll come home rejuvenated, and Bobby will say, "You need to rest. You've been gone all day."

To which I respond, "I just did."

Takeaways

- Find your happy place.
- Listen to your body when it says to slow down.
- Everyone finds rest in a different way.

LET'S TAKE ACTION: What makes you feel recharged?

____

____

____

____

SO SCARED I ALMOST THREW UP

I may be traumatized, but now I have bragging rights for life. I chickened out two years earlier, but I finally did it—I HIKED ANGELS LANDING! It's a famous Rock formation in Utah and one of the top 5 most dangerous hikes in the world. Bobby and I were celebrating 26 years of marriage, so we returned to one of our favorite places, Zion National Park.

We started at dawn. It took us just over 4 hours, and walking up is so freaking hard. But I was mentally prepared (though I should have physically prepared more) and made it to the top. The Angels Landing part is pretty brutal. You think you're almost there, then you're not. It's a mental and physical challenge and should not be taken lightly. There's one part where it drops over 1,000 ft. on each side. Believe it or not, that wasn't what scared me. The worst part was the side edges walking up with the chains. Bobby was so patient and helped me the entire way. (He had already hiked Angels Landing when I chickened out last time, so he had some practice.) I've never had such an intense, proud feeling of doing something so strenuous and terrifying. And it's up to you. Nobody is going to do it for you; you have to earn it.

What seemed so scary going up was way easier coming back down. It makes me think of marriage, business, and life in general. Things that are new to us will always be terrifying at first, but as we get used to doing them, they become easier. We make goals and plan dreams, but we still have to take action.

Thanks, Bobby, for being my "ride-or-die," my rock today on top of a big ass rock, AND for being married to the crazy for so many years.

Takeaways

- You are stronger and braver than you think.
- Things will always be scarier the first time you do them.
- You need to take action to create the life you want.

LET'S TAKE ACTION: Name a time when you did something really challenging physically. How did you feel when you were done?

____

____

____

____

EXPECT THINGS TO GO WELL

Life is full of people who either expect the worst or the best. I recommend the latter. Going through life expecting things to be good is much more enjoyable. Someone once told me they don't want to do that because they don't want to be disappointed. But here's the thing: if you were around in 2020, we were all disappointed. From canceled high school graduations and weddings to being isolated from friends and family, plans changed, vacations postponed, businesses shut down, low toilet paper supply, and, worst of all, many of us lost family members. We have been and will continue to be disappointed. It will happen. So, instead of living life that way, how about adopting a different attitude? Expect things to go well. I've been living this way for quite a while.

My daughter calls it magic. When I pull into a parking lot, I immediately look for close parking because I know someone will pull out at just the right time. The other day, I got something stuck in my bottom permanent retainer. It always traps food, and I hate that thing. Anyway, I needed floss. I went downstairs to the front desk of the hotel I was staying at, and they didn't have any floss. Instead of accepting my fate, I expected good things to happen. I asked, "Do you have a toothpick, anything? This is driving me nuts."

She said, "Hold on!" Then she grabbed a key, opened up the coffee shop next door, and returned with a mint-flavored toothpick! "Magic," my daughter says. "Magic."

Expect good things to happen, and more often than not, you'll start to see the magic too!

Takeaways

- Expect good things to happen.
- Be the glass-half-full person.

LET'S TAKE ACTION: I challenge you—wait, I double-dog dare you—to expect things to go well this week. Try having the attitude that things WILL go well. When they do, come back and write about it.

___

___

___

___

REALLY ASK

My friend Rita is one of the kindest people I have ever met. She and her husband, Mr. Potter, are more than just friends; I really feel like they are family. One of the many kind things Rita does is ask the grocery store clerk how they are doing. She doesn't just say hi; she looks them in the eye and genuinely asks them how they are doing, and she really wants to know. Inspired by her, I started adopting this approach.

One day, I witnessed the power of kindness through this simple gesture. The guy in front of me at the checkout immediately complained to the cashier about the store not carrying his preferred brand of beer in bottles. He was really rude, and the cashier was visibly upset by his attitude. She did the bare minimum to quickly get him checked out and on his way. When it was my turn, I greeted her with, "Hi, how's your day? I hope it's going well!"

She stopped and looked at me, shocked that I took a moment to acknowledge her. She said her day was good, and we had a short conversation about the day. She helped bag my groceries, we wished each other well, and we both walked away smiling.

The interesting thing about this is that the mean guy and I performed the same action in life (checking out groceries) but had totally different experiences. He left angry, and I left happy. He left being mean to others, and I left excited to talk to another person.

Be mindful of how you treat the people around you. They may be background characters in your life, but remember, they are the leading role in their own lives and deserve to be treated as such.

Takeaways

- The same experiences can yield totally different results based on your attitude.
- Always treat others with kindness.

LET'S TAKE ACTION: Ask the next person who checks you out at a grocery store, department store, or wherever, "How is your day?" And really mean it! What was their reaction? How did you feel? (It does feel weird at first, but it gets easier and more fun.)

____

____

____

____

COULDN'T PUT ON MY SHOES OR MY PANTS

It's conference time, and I'm here with two of my friends, learning about business strategy. It's one of my favorite times of the year. This year, I'm being honored on stage, and I'm so excited! This particular conference really went all out. They rented out Sea World just for our group—an entire theme park opened just for us! We enjoyed endless rides without lines, free drinks, food, and even got our caricatures drawn, my friend Gretchen and I posing for fun. I'm thrilled!

After a quick change into jeans, I'm ready to go, but then, in a split second, my back pops. Something is terribly wrong. I am stuck and can't put on my shoes. Terrified, I managed to get them on slowly, and we headed to SeaWorld. I have to walk slowly, and by the time we get back to the room, I'm in so much pain. My friend Mindy, whose husband is a chiropractor in Florida, has some contacts in the area. Expecting the best, she thankfully sets me up with a chiropractor about an hour away from Orlando. I take an Uber to the appointment and spend the next three days going back and forth to the chiropractor, trying to get some relief. I miss much of the conference, and I'm in tears because tonight is the night of the big award.

I look at my friends and say, "I can't go on stage wearing shorts and a hoodie."

I start crying, and they immediately say, "We're all moms; we will help you get dressed."

I'm like, "Friends shouldn't have to do this." In tears and not wanting to miss the awards, I manage to take a shower and slowly get dressed. I'm able to get my boots on and throw a hat over my unwashed hair. My friends helped me, and I made it to the award ceremony.

The point of this story is that your life NEEDS to have friends! Yes, it takes work and mainly time to build friendships, but it's ALWAYS worth it! You never know when you'll need a friend to help you get dressed so they can cheer you on when you receive a major award (like a leg lamp, but cooler).

Takeaways

- Don't just be the friend who needs her pants put on. Be willing to be the friend who can help put on the pants.
- Nurture the friendships you have.

LET'S TAKE ACTION: List the friends who would help put your pants on in times of need.

____

____

____

____

A MAN AMONGST MEN

Same activity, but two completely different experiences! We live on a golf course and see all the golfers from our house. It's the best spot for people-watching. While I drink my coffee, I witness both massive success and failure on the golf course. I've seen grown men kick trees, throw their clubs, curse at the sky, and pretty much everything in between. One day, I saw a man hit his golf ball into the trees and then have a "come to Jesus" moment, cursing the ball as he decided life was against him. A few minutes later, another guy came to take his shot. It landed right in the middle of the fairway. Moments later, his friend started screaming at the top of his lungs with hands stretched wide towards the sky, "YOU'RE A MAN AMONGST MEN!"

I looked at Pixie, and we laughed. "He's a man amongst men? What the heck does that mean?"

The guy jumped onto his golf cart and drove off, feeling like a million bucks. It made me realize how one man was hating life while another was celebrating it. Both were playing golf but having two totally different experiences! Who you surround yourself with can help your confidence. Be careful not to be with people who take you to the "Suck Zone."

Takeaways

- Who you surround yourself with will make a day fun or dreadful.
- Words are powerful.

LET'S TAKE ACTION: What is something in your life that you could turn into a better experience?

____

____

____

____

SMILING'S MY FAVORITE

Elf is one of my favorite movies. I haven't come across anyone who hasn't seen this movie. If you haven't, please stop reading this book and go watch *Elf* right now.

Now that you've seen it let's proceed. Anyway, in the movie, there's a part where Will Ferrell, the actor who stars as the main character, says, "Smiling's my favorite." I've used this quote many times, and you probably have as well, or at least heard someone use it. My goal for you is to smile at other people when you walk by, not in a creepy way, but just in a kind way. Now, this may be hard to do if you are in New York City.

When I was in my early 20s, my mother-in-law invited me to go with her to New York City. She was there on business, and I got to roam the city while she was working. While roaming, I came across the MTV studios and saw a long line. Being the curious person I am, I asked what the line was for. It was for a taping of *Total Request Live* (TRL), a show I watched regularly. I mean, Host Carson Daly and superstars being interviewed! I'm in! So, I waited in line and got chosen to go in for the filming.

I was inside MTV studios while Usher was being interviewed about 5 feet away from me. I still remember the lime green shirt I was wearing that day. It was in April, so it was chilly outside. They took our coats and cell phones while they were shooting. It felt so surreal. This was one of the first times I felt independent, and I loved that feeling! No one knew where I was. I wasn't trying to document it with a smartphone. I was just in the moment, watching Usher do some dance moves. It was awesome!

Coming off the high of MTV, I tried to find my way back to the hotel. This was WAY before phones were "smart." There was no GPS capability. The texting feature on my phone was still numbers. If you know, you know. I was lost and trying to find my way back to the hotel. As I walked by people on the streets of New York City, I would look at them and smile. About five people in, I realized that this was not the same standard as back home. Raised in Texas, you not only smile, but you also ask how they are doing. This was not the place.

The next day, it was raining in New York City, and I bought an umbrella. As I walked the streets, I would start to smile at someone, then look down and start laughing because it made me uncomfortable. Then I realized that just because people weren't smiling back at me didn't mean they were trying to be unkind. Sometimes, it's simply the way different parts of the world operate.

Takeaways

- Be curious and willing to explore.
- Don't judge others.

LET'S TAKE ACTION: When is a time you could have given someone the benefit of the doubt?

____

____

____

____

JUMP OUT OF THE POOL

Swim aerobics at the YMCA took up a few months of my life. My mother-in-law and I would meet at the "Y" to get in shape. She was struggling with knee issues, so this low-impact activity was perfect. I love water, so I was in! Being the youngest in the pool, I always felt like I had an advantage. I could swim forever, so sometimes I would do the exercises in the deep end just to challenge myself. Remember, I'm a self-proclaimed mermaid. One day, as we were swimming, I had an idea! It was like a light bulb went off in the pool. The class was only about 20 minutes in, but the idea struck me, and I had to act on it! I jumped out of the pool and headed home to my computer. By the end of the afternoon, I had made over $1100.

The value of taking action before your brain catches up can help you create the life you want. If I had stayed in the pool and continued with my normal routine, I wouldn't have pushed myself to make $1100 that day. Although that was a big win for me, it also showed me what I could achieve in a short amount of time.

Takeaways

- Take action before the idea leaves you.
- When inspiration strikes, be ready to seize it.
- Always have a notepad around.

LET'S TAKE ACTION: Take action as soon as you have the idea! Do you have an idea right now that you could pursue?

____

____

____

____

POSTERBOARD BUDGETS

Years after leaving my full-time teaching job and pursuing my business full time, I was burned out. Bobby came home from work and found me filling out applications for a local high school art teacher position, tears streaming down my face as I typed. I was ready to quit when he sat on the floor beside me and said, "You can't stop."

I had been at this business thing for a while, but it just felt like no matter how much I moved forward, I wasn't getting anywhere. I was burning the candle at both ends and was not getting the results I expected. The teaching salary would have been $47,000 a year—dependable, consistent. But that day, my sweet husband believed in me more than I believed in myself.

We decided to track every single cent we would spend for the next month. He's more of a digital-type tracker, but I needed everything written on a posterboard. We agreed to meet every week and write down everything that was going into our account and everything that was going out. Within a few weeks, we realized that we were overspending. We also realized that I would have lost money if I had taken a teaching position. I was actually making double what I would have been making as a teacher; I just didn't know it because we weren't tracking it. Once I saw the numbers plain as day, I decided going back to teaching wasn't an option. It was "game on," now that I knew.

We sometimes slide back into old habits, and I always bring the posterboard back out to get us back on track. Since we do this, we are able to plan ahead and do the things we really want to.

Takeaways

- Track your spending in detail, down to the penny, so you can channel it toward the dreams and goals you have in life.
- Get your posterboards out! Whether it's a tracking app like Every Dollar from Ramsey Solutions or old-school posterboard writing, just do it. Use the tools that work best for you. Your future will thank you.

LET'S TAKE ACTION: Write out how this posterboard method could help you. If not, what is another way you can organize your finances?

____

____

____

____

ALWAYS GET BACK UP

Life will knock you down over and over again. The only choice is to get back up. It doesn't mean you have to be overly optimistic, but there's something to be said for choosing joy even when you're sad. It sometimes sounds like a country song: "*Lost my truck, and my dog...*" It's easy to go through life counting deaths, surgeries, bankruptcy, relationship trials, and so much more. Then, I remember all the good. Death brings a new appreciation for everything. Surgeries heal, bankruptcies teach lessons, relationships bring grace and acceptance, and losing pets always teaches unconditional love. We all have moments when life tries to chip away at us. But you have to find the joy. Whatever you are going through right now, I'm so sorry. It's a part of the ride life brings us. It's not all good, but it's real. Pixie shared this scripture with me, and I think it's perfect to remember:

Romans 8:18, "For I consider that the sufferings of this present time are not worth comparing with the glory that is to be revealed to us."

Whatever you're going through, I hope you find the lessons and some peace in whatever season you're in.

Takeaways

- Find the joy.
- Trust God's plan.

LET'S TAKE ACTION: What is something that has happened in your life that ultimately turned out for the better? How did you feel during the situation? What was your reaction after you realized it ended up being good?

____

____

____

____

GRIEF IS A STRANGE BEAST

Having a hysterectomy on the one-year anniversary of my mom's death is tough. It's the kind of surgery you want your mom around for. She was always the best at saying everything would be okay. A few days before my surgery, my dad texted me to reassure me that it would all be okay. He's doing a great job of stepping in and trying to fill the void left by our mom. He's got a lot on his plate, and phone calls to our mom were one of the big things all five of us did consistently. We all called her—some of us daily, others weekly—but one of the things I miss most is knowing she would always answer. By the way our voice sounded, she instantly knew what mood we were in and what to say.

Grief is a strange beast. I've been told it will get easier by some and also told it never gets easier by others. I'm choosing to believe that it will get easier. Although some moments are really hard, I want and need my life to reflect joy, even through the extremely sad times.

When you're building your business, or even several years in, there will be some really tough days. You will go through challenges, including the hardest ones, like losing the people you love most. Remember, no matter what happens in your life, take the time you need and then get back to doing what you do best. Everyone is different, and everyone handles situations differently, but for me, I had to get back to work. It was an escape from so much sadness. By focusing on others, I was able to take a mental break from the pain of loss. You can always go back to that dream, that goal you had for yourself. So, instead of punishing yourself by allowing setbacks and life to give you an excuse to give up, use it as fuel. Take the time you need to grieve, but then use that to fuel you to live the life you want.

Takeaways

- Take time to grieve.
- It's okay to put your dreams on hold as long as you go back.
- Channel the struggles of life to move you forward.
- Help someone who is going through the same struggle.

LET'S TAKE ACTION: What is a hard time you've gone through, and how did you get through it? Is there something you are allowing to be an excuse not to move forward? (Be honest with yourself.)

____

____

____

____

PEOPLE ARE JUST PEOPLE

I watched the movie *Paper Towns*. It flooded my mind with tons of memories from high school: having fun with friends, being silly, laughing all the time, taking risks and chances, and not being afraid to mess up. Falling madly in love with my boyfriend at the time, now my husband of 26 years, reminds me of how glad I am that he took a chance with me. We are all trying to make our way in this world, and sometimes we forget to take chances or make mistakes like we did when we were young. They mention in the movie that it's a treacherous thing to believe that a person is more than just a person. People are just people.

He also talked about noticing those times when they are great and having gratitude for those moments. In my teens and twenties, I wasn't so good at that. Now, I try to be more present, and I feel it really does make a difference in my life. People are just people, but we each get to choose how we want to live each day. We get to choose our thoughts, and in turn, our thoughts shape our reality.

I know that my life has been full of mistakes, fears, anxiety, and tons of doubt. But I also realize and know that my life has tons of excitement, opportunity, fun, laughter, joy, and love. I know that by appreciating all that I am given, I can fully commit to new things without the fear of failure, without the fear of messing up, without the fear of not being good enough.

What are your fears? Are you able to be grateful for what you have today? Put gratitude first! It's amazing what happens in your day when you are thankful first. This applies to your thoughts as well, not just what you say but what you think. Monitor your thoughts, and maybe, just maybe, your outcome will change. Your reality will change. Your attitude will change.

With your attitude, you can help others. Isn't that why we are all here in the first place—to help others?

Takeaways

- People are just people.
- Monitor your thoughts, and your reality will change.

LET'S TAKE ACTION: Choose a new thought today. What is a thought that doesn't come naturally but you know will help you have a better attitude about life? Write it down.

____

____

____

____

HEART TRANSPLANT

It's Sunday, March 12th, and I have over 25 kids, plus another seven or so grandparents, ready to paint. All the kids are seated and excited to get started. As I am about to begin, my phone rings. It's one of my brothers, so I send it to voicemail. About 10 seconds later, it's my mom calling. I immediately send it to voicemail, and then my heart starts beating fast. Within another minute, it rings again, and it's my husband.

I know what the call is about before I answer. I quickly answer in a room full of anxiously waiting kids and say, "It's here, isn't it… is it for real???"

"Yes, it's time," Bobby says.

I start crying on the phone in a room full of strangers and say, "Please get everything ready. I'll be there as soon as the party is over, and we can drive to Austin!"

He says calmly, "I'm already packing. I'll have everything ready, so when you are here, we can go."

I hang up the phone, look at Pixie, and say, "Poppy is getting his heart today!!!"

I take a deep breath and then get the audience's attention. I introduce myself and say, "I just got the call after 22 months of waiting that my dad is receiving his heart transplant today!"

I'm, of course, in tears. "So, as soon as I'm done teaching this fun painting, I'm heading to Austin, but I LOVE to PAINT, so right now, we are going to PAINT! Who's ready to paint!?"

The kids are excited and, of course, say yes, they are ready! We start the painting.

I notice a few of the grandparents with tears in their eyes as well. They understand what's going on, what this Sunday afternoon phone call meant to me and my family. We finished the painting, and surprisingly, I only had tears a few times when one of the adults would mention it and give me a hug. It was all tears of happiness!

After the last person left, I called my mom and dad, and they were on their way to the hospital. Surgery would be happening soon, and he was so happy. Sad, of course, for the donor and their family, but very happy he gets a second chance at life. I tell him I love him and hope to see him before he goes into surgery.

We arrive at the house, and Bobby has everything ready. Our dog Blue has even been taken to Bobby's mom's house so we can leave immediately. He is such an amazing man. I can't believe he's my husband. He packed everything, from my heating blanket (I don't go anywhere without it) to cash and even snacks for the car ride.

I'm still in shock that we got the call after so many months of waiting. Although I prayed every night for my dad to get better and receive a new heart, doubts started to creep in as he continued to lose weight and spend more time in bed. The drive to Austin was filled with gratitude! I just couldn't believe it was all happening, and to MY family. We get our dad back!

We are in Austin. I tell Pixie to have everything ready so we can get out of the car as quickly as possible and make it to the room. We might have time to see him before he's taken back.

It was crazy, almost like something out of a movie in slow motion. We round the corner and rush to his room. Within 10 minutes of our arrival, he is wheeled out for an all-night surgery. I was so happy to hug him and tell him I loved him before the surgery. When I arrived, two of my brothers, my sister-in-law, and my cousin were already there. He had a packed house, and he was READY!

The nurse suggested we take a picture. We were all hesitant at first, but I'm so glad she insisted. That picture captured how happy he was. I had never seen him glow like that before. He's a fighter, and in that photo, you can tell he will come back better than ever.

Now, the wait begins. We all head to the waiting room, and within a few hours, my third brother shows up from Florida. He took a flight as soon as he heard. If you know my family, the all-nighter was spent with tons of laughter and maybe a few inappropriate jokes. Eventually, we all become delirious, and things just continue to get funnier as the night goes on. Just the way my dad would expect it!

Finally, 7 a.m. hit on March 13th, 2017. The doctor comes in to tell us how the surgery went. He calmly describes removing the defibrillator, the VAD (Ventricular assist device), and then the heart… I interrupt, "Wait… What was in him?"

He replies, "Oh, he was on a bypass machine."

As a visual person, all I could picture was my dad lying there with his entire body cut open and NO HEART inside him! What???

Then the doctor says, "We put the new heart in, and it just starts beating on its own."

After hearing this, I am in shock. It's such a miracle that someone took the time to sign up to be a donor, and then, after the saddest day in their family, it became the happiest day in ours.

I am so grateful for that young man who decided to be a donor. I'm thankful for today's medical miracles and how doctors can perform such procedures! I'm also thankful that my mom and dad now have a future that hopefully doesn't just involve doctor appointments and resting. They have a second chance, and we all have our dad back!

Many things happened in the days that followed. Too many to share here, and with a clouded, sleep-deprived brain, I may not remember it all correctly. But I do remember a few days after the surgery, we were sitting in my dad's room. He was still sedated and on a ventilator. The nurse came in, and I noticed her listening to his heartbeat.

I asked, "Is it possible for us to listen to his new heart?"

She checked to make sure it was okay, then said, "Yes, it's fine."

This moment was unreal! It felt like when I first heard Pixie's heartbeat when I was pregnant. It was this moment of knowing my dad would be okay. Yes, he didn't look so okay, but we had seen him like this before, and we knew he was a fighter… AND THIS HEART WAS BEATING AT 107 BPM! It was WORKING!!!

We listen to his new heart, donated by someone else.

We listen and know there is a future for him and for us.

We listen, knowing there will be a change in our family forever.

We listen knowing that the donor's sacrifice will not be in vain.

It was a miracle, and I couldn't be more thankful to all the donors out there, especially this one. I am so thankful for him and his family.

As people prayed for my dad and all my family, I couldn't help but think that this was the BEST SPRING BREAK OF MY LIFE! It was exhausting but a wonderful, answered prayer of exhaustion. I will always remember this Spring Break and the call I received on March 12th. I will never forget how God gives miracles. Since then, my prayers have been bigger and bolder. I've always known that God can do anything, but now I've seen it firsthand. I'm not putting Him in a box anymore. I know that He wants the best for us, and I've seen His work firsthand in my family.

I hope that you take time to be grateful and never lose hope. We waited 22 months for a heart transplant, and now we can say that my dad is recovered. I am so thankful I can beat him at basketball and have many more fun times together.

Our job on this earth is to love people, serve others, and always choose joy, even when times are hard. I am so grateful to be able to say that we are choosing joy, even when times are hard! I hope this story helps you. Don't lose hope.

Takeaways

- Choose joy when times are hard.
- Never lose hope.
- Consider being a donor.

LET'S TAKE ACTION: Is there a time in your life when you lost hope? What's something you are hopeful for in the coming months?

____

____

____

____

I DIDN'T LIKE MY BABY

Yes, I said it... I didn't like my baby. But before you get all crazy, read the whole story.

Pixie is graduating, but it seemed like yesterday she was a colicky baby who I loved but honestly didn't like so much at the time. Sixteen hours a day of crying for over six months straight was driving me insane! My hubby and I typed up a Matrimonial Saving Schedule where everything was planned out to the minute, including who would have Pixie at what time, so that we wouldn't get divorced or bail on each other in the first year of parenthood.

Either we weren't listening, or no one told us (I'm pretty sure it was the first one) that being a parent would change everything. Bobby and I had been married for nine years before I got pregnant with Pixie. Our life was on our schedule. I worked full-time and went to school full-time, and I thought I would throw parenting in there as one of my jobs or hobbies. Boy, was I awakened! Like for a whole year! We felt robbed of the perfect birthing experience, having an emergency C-section and Pixie in the NICU; we didn't see her for hours. I always hear women talk about their babies sleeping through the night, how breastfeeding was so easy, and what a joy it was. I just smile, keeping my story to a minimum so as not to put a damper on the joys of motherhood.

Then I smile again because I can.

No, seriously, a week after having Pixie, my face stopped working, and I had to wear an eye patch because my left eye wouldn't blink! After finding out it was Bell's Palsy, my family did what we do best: made tons of pirate jokes and asked me to try and whistle. Christmas that year was met with SURPRISE! A deck of cards with my face on them, trying to smile. Oh, and a mug to make sure my face was imprinted forever.

So, with a crying baby, a face that stopped working, being forced to bottle-feed because of all the steroids the emergency room put me on, and no sleep for almost a year, we called it "the zombie year." By the grace of God, we managed to keep our little Pixie alive as we tried to figure out how to parent. For the moms out there with babies that sleep through the night, count your blessings and enjoy your sleep. I pray all new moms have the "sleeping through the night" babies! I know you think I'm the worst parent in the world. I'm writing the truth to those new moms out there who may be thinking, *PARENTING IS HARD!* Yes, it is hard, but SO, SO WORTH IT!

I would do it all over again in a heartbeat! I had no idea how much I would fall in love with this little girl we named Pixie. I had no idea that the same girl who cried for hours straight would also make me laugh every day. I had no idea that the little baby who wouldn't smile would become the most joyful child I've ever met. I had no idea that she would turn out to be a way better person than Bobby and I combined. I had no idea she would make me feel so much love and so much excitement about life. I had no idea that this baby would be the best thing that has ever happened to Bobby and I.

The biggest gift I'll ever receive.

The greatest person I've ever met.

I'm so thankful to be her mom.

Takeaways

- Parenting can be hard, but always worth it.
- The days are long, but the years are short.
- Every part of life has seasons. If you are in a hard stage of life right now, it will change.
- The only constant is change.

LET'S TAKE ACTION: What's something you struggled with but are now grateful for?

____

____

____

____

SOMETIMES I FEEL LIKE I WASN'T MEANT TO BE A PARENT

I was a teacher for ten years, so I got my fill of kids. My daughter is the best! She's a really good kid, and I'm not just saying that—I've taught thousands of kids, so I really have thousands to compare her to. However, sometimes I just want a minute!

Several years ago, I vividly remember a situation where I needed a pause. We were grocery shopping, and I listened to all her stories as we went through the store. We played car games on the way home, talked over some homework project plans, discussed why people sometimes wear certain things (we saw an interesting outfit at the grocery store), and many other things. We started putting groceries away, and now she has burst into song. The dog is jumping around, needing to go outside; my hands are overloaded with plastic grocery bags; and my daughter is in her own little world, probably on a Broadway stage somewhere.

I mean, how long can someone actually use their vocal cords?

At that moment, all the frustration from the day and my patience for the last two hours came bolting out. "Pixie! I need a break! Please, STOP!" In her cute little head, she sees nothing wrong.

However, my creative brain is constantly making lists, organizing the evening's dinner plans, remembering something that has to go in the mail, etc. You moms know the drill. So, for a second, I feel really bad. I grab an adult beverage from the fridge and let her go to her room while I finish putting up groceries in silence. My brain starts to think that maybe I wasn't meant to be a parent.

But then the next day...

My daughter comes into the art studio and asks, "What can I do to help you?"

And I say, "Oh my gosh, I really need help. You don't mind?"

She says, "It's the least I can do for you being such a great mom!"

My heart melts, and I am SO THANKFUL to be a parent! So thankful to be HER MOM! I hug her and thank her, and then I put her straight to work! I'll hold onto that comment the next time my daughter is in full-force performance mode for her version of the musical *Wicked.*

The whole point of this story is to remind you to take time for yourself. Take time to do the things you love, so you don't end up bitter and overworked. Our SOUL needs it! Our husband needs it, and especially our little ones looking up to us need it!

My soul needs art, painting especially. There is nothing better than spending an hour in Michaels buying fun new paints and then heading home for an afternoon of creating. Find what speaks to you.

Takeaways

- Be patient.
- Take time for yourself.

LET'S TAKE ACTION: Where in your schedule can you set aside a few minutes for yourself? Write down a day of the week where you can set aside 30 minutes to 1 hour to just be by yourself.

____

____

____

____

TAKE ACTION THROUGH FEAR

What are you terrified of? I know you have something you're scared of, but maybe you're afraid to admit it to yourself or others. Well, the girl below is me, and I used to be terrified of everything! I got married as soon as I turned 18, and Bobby used to work late. Coming from a big family, I was ALWAYS surrounded by people. I used to call my mom at night while Bobby was working and lay on the couch covered in blankets, trying to be as quiet as possible. I was so terrified someone was going to break in and attack me. Can you relate?

The same thing happened with driving on big roads. I was TERRIFIED! I would almost close my eyes as I approached freeways, and Bobby would frantically yell, "WATCH THE ROAD!" The merge was the scariest.

Fast forward a couple of decades, and I'm not scared of much. I owe it all to lots of bumps and bruises, disappointments, blood, sweat, tears, health scares, losses, failures—so many failures! You see, our past is important. It shows us how far we've come. It helps us measure our success moving forward. It shows how strong we are and what we can endure if we just keep moving forward. Thinking about the next 10 years of my life, I am looking forward to conquering more goals but with way less fear. Having been there before, I know for certain FEAR is a LIAR! What's holding you back? What do you want to accomplish this year or even this next decade?

Let's remember that God is in control, and if we put our trust in Him, He can use us to do amazing, wonderful things on this earth.

Takeaways

- Let's be fearless!

- Let's set impossible goals!
- Do it all for God's glory!

WHO'S WITH ME?

LET'S TAKE ACTION: What's holding you back from going after your dreams?

____

____

____

____

SENSITIVE SOUL

It's one of those rare moments when I'm deep in thought, just enjoying putting color on paper. No Social Media Lives, no talking, just a time-lapse going as I blast some praise music. It's not an intense project, just crayons and watercolor. But there's something about blasting some praise music, drinking some coffee, and just enjoying the process. I'm so thankful that in all the craziness of the world, we have a place to escape and let our minds wander.

I just wanted to take a minute to speak to all the artists out there. We are a sensitive bunch of folks. It's not that other people don't feel or care, but something about our creative spirit makes us highly in tune with others' feelings and fears. At the same time, it also makes us question our own self-worth. Our own fears sneak up on us and try to haunt us with words of self-doubt and thoughts like, *Who am I to be doing this? Who am I to succeed?* What I've learned as an artist, as a human, and as a person who has felt all of those things more times than I'd like to admit, is that those feelings CANNOT define us. We can't let self-doubt creep in and ruin the hope we have for the future.

We are about to hit our 6-year anniversary in May with over 3,000 members, and even as my membership grew, I had those feelings of self-doubt bubble up. What I have really learned is that taking action through fear is the only way to go. At the end of the day, we are all scared. Scared of failure, scared of rejection, scared of feeling lost, scared of losing hope. But we have to take action regardless, continually moving forward. Having a bankruptcy years ago and that overwhelming feeling of not being worthy of success because I screwed up so badly followed me for a long time. It still can creep up now if I let it. Then I remember I have to put my faith in God, know how to help my members and keep getting back up and trying again. And again. Entrepreneurship is NOT for the weak. It's hard. But it's so worth it.

So here I sit in an art studio bigger than I ever dreamed, so thankful God gave me the wisdom to find several ways to make money so I hopefully never find myself back in that position ever again. Learning more and more about how I can help others have bigger wins is what drives me to be better, learn more, and help them achieve success. And in turn, they have been the biggest blessing in my family's life. I love having a business and the people we help so much, and I still can't believe how much life has changed in just a short time.

Don't lose hope!

Don't ever compare!

Don't give up!

And failure is a part of it. My new motto is "The faster I fail, the faster I get up." Fail fast, and then fail again until you get it right. I promise you will be so thankful you didn't give up.

Takeaways

- Fail fast.
- Fail often.

LET'S TAKE ACTION: What is something you know you are supposed to do, but have given up on in the past? Take a moment to write a quote that inspires you to take action and tack it to your wall so you can see it every day! I would LOVE to see it! Send me a DM on Instagram @texasartandsoul_, and I can share it in my stories!

____

____

____

____

CAN I TELL YOU SOMETHING?

One last thing. Don't give up. Building a life that you love can be hard, but I want you to think of it this way: I'm going to do one thing this week to make my life more creative and joyful. Then, next week, I'll do another thing to bring joy into my life. I have seen so many people with so much passion in their hearts, knowing God has led them to do something for a reason, and then they give up at the first sign of rejection.

You will be told no.

You will get frustrated.

You will be overwhelmed.

But... if you just commit to this with the good and the bad, I promise you that you will grow! You will gain a ton of confidence! You will realize that failure is a GIANT part of success. You will take more chances and know that God has a plan! You will succeed in building a creatively beautiful life that you love.

So stop thinking that it all has to be built in one day. Just concentrate on doing one thing at a time. Then, guess what happens? Your confidence will start to grow. You'll hit some walls—totally normal. You'll think, *This isn't for me, who am I to do this?* Again, it's totally normal! Then, you'll have a win!

Keep praying for opportunities, and then take action through fear! And when you get overwhelmed, confused, or even lost, just take a deep breath, go for a walk, say a prayer, and ask for support. Hang in there and keep trying. Or should I say, hang in there and keep failing! Because the faster you fail, the faster you succeed!

I am here to believe in you in case you don't believe in yourself. People have done that for me, and I want to do that for you.

Always remember, you are magically made, overly optimistic, and perfectly placed.

Heidi

Want to learn more?

Visit www.texasartandsoul.com

ACKNOWLEDGMENTS

Bobby, you believe in me more than I believe in myself. You're my soulmate, my "ride-or-die," and the sexiest man alive. Thank you for not only allowing me to chase my big, crazy dreams, but also supporting them in every way possible. I love you so much, and I'm so thankful to have you in my life. They say marriage is like an endless sleepover with your favorite weirdo—that is definitely us! Your endless hobbies keep my life interesting, and I'm so grateful for it. Thank you for keeping me stable when life happens and rocking my world when I need an adventure.

Pixie, for always being a little clingy and willing to bounce ideas around and talk about our crazy dreams. You are WAY more talented than I will ever be, and I'm so thankful to be your mom and watch you chase your own dreams. I can't wait to get matching tattoos and travel all around the world with you. You are a better daughter than I could have ever imagined. Thank you for shopping till we drop, creating till 3 a.m., and always wanting to hang out with me. I love you so so much!

My dad, the real Rod Stewart, you are always ready to jump in and help with anything from our events to cutting out surfboards. You always remind me that I'm on the right track and that I'm a doer (just like YOU). Your hugs are THE BEST. And don't worry, I won't tell the other siblings that I'm your favorite. Thank you for raising me with an adventurous spirit and kind soul. I would never be who I am without you.

My mom, I miss you so much. Sometimes, I wish I could have one last phone call with you to tell you I love you. Thank you for always letting me fall apart when I would call and telling me that it would be okay.

Cherie, I won the lottery of mother-in-laws with you. Thank you for always seeing the crazy in me and jumping in full force! You kept me dreaming when I thought I couldn't, and you reminded me that God is always on my side.

Eddie, thank you for believing in my dreams and always stepping in to help me. From business strategy to the "not taking the last beer" rule, you have helped me in so many places in my life. I appreciate you more than you will ever know.

To my sister Nikka, I'm forever grateful for the many days we laid on the beach and dreamed about our futures. I'm also forever grateful for your salsa; please never stop making it.

To my brothers: Mike, thank you for being my biggest fan and always supporting my art, from painting murals at your home, school, and the pieces hanging on your wall (the heart is in your painting).

David, thank you for keeping me laughing with Zoltar and teaching me not to take life too seriously.

Josh, thank you for always having a cool song to play on your guitar and being such a great listener.

Thank y'all for keeping me laughing anytime we are together. God gave me the coolest siblings ever, and I love y'all so much.

Gma Evelyn, thank you for skydiving with us, jumping on trampolines, letting us pick strawberries, and always being so sweet to me. I'll never forget the night you helped me with a paint party, and we laughed and laughed. You always told me that I work so hard, but you've always been such a great example of that.

Alyson, the girl with the clipboard and one of my favorite people in the world. You are not only willing to listen to my crazy ideas like renting a horse or putting on a circus, but you also find the tent! Thank you for making my dreams come to life. You've been a part of my story since before the surfboard days. Your endless hours of supporting me will never be forgotten, and I'm so thankful for you.

To my friend Mindy, I always look forward to our endless talks about our business and dreams. Thank you for being such a light in the world and praying for me when I needed it the most. From the Everett lunch tables to our FaceTime dinner tables, you have helped me in so many ways. Thank you for a wonderful friendship.

To Tamara, Sarah, Brandie, Kasey, Cindy, Christie, and Gretchen. Your friendship came at the perfect time in my life. Without your loud and crazy personalities, growing my company wouldn't have been nearly as fun. Your inspiring and "get stuff done" attitude has always pushed me forward. I treasure our meetups and late-night talks. Thank you for always believing in me. Being just a text or a quick call away is such a lifeline.

To my FB angel, Gretchen. Thank you for always believing in me and for spending hours and hours talking about funnels! You are a massive part of why this business has grown so much, and I'm forever grateful to you!

Rita and Mr. Potter, you both are such a joy to have in my life. Thank you for allowing Pixie and me to stay with you during our paint party adventures. Rita, thank you for showing us that the adventure never stops. Mr. Potter, thank you for your entertaining clogging and your beautiful pottery. You are the best chosen family we could ask for, and we are so grateful to have you in our lives.

To all the Paint Party Headquarters members, I am forever grateful for your trust in me and my team. Without you, we wouldn't be able to keep dreaming up these crazy ideas! It's such an honor to cheer you on and watch your businesses grow. Thank you for bringing all the joy and fun to our amazing group. I am endlessly thankful for your kind hearts and beautiful souls.

To my team, a gazillion thanks for helping to grow this magical, enchanting, crazy, and wild dream. Your work ethic is unmatched, and your ability to help so many people is forever appreciated. Thank you for staying by my side through the ups and downs of entrepreneurship, and ultimately, thank you for being my friends.

To all my paint party people, I am so grateful that you allow me and my family into your homes, churches, community centers, and many other places. Thank you for always supporting our business and allowing us to be a part of your lives.

To Cris, thank you for believing in me before I even wrote this book. Our stories have been so similar, and I'm surprised our paths never crossed until a couple of years ago. Thank you for raving with me over funnels and crazy traveling. Thank you for making this book everything I hoped it would be.

Finally, to the One who created me to dream: I thank God for everything He has done in my life. From my family to my business, He has led me through it all. I thank Him for the talents He has provided me with and the ability to push through hard times. Life has its highs and lows, and with God by my side, it's easier for me to endure. Thank you for believing in me when I struggled to trust Your plan. As I move into the next chapter of my life, I trust that whatever You have in store for me and my family is magically made, overly optimistic, and perfectly placed.

THANK YOU FOR READING MY BOOK!

Just to say thanks for buying and reading my book, I would love to help you with your creative adventures! Check out my website below for ways to connect.

Simply Scan the QR Code Here:

I appreciate your interest in my book and value your feedback as it helps me improve w future versions. I would appreciate it if you could leave your invaluable review on Amazon.com with your feedback.

Made in the USA
Columbia, SC
07 February 2024